For George & Trish

God Bless You

GW00326573

Being Yourself in Jesus
and He's being Himself in You

by

Colin Shewry

Insightsfor...publishing

Contents

Acknowledgements

There are so many people to thank; which just goes to show what we can achieve by working together!

Firstly of course, I thank God, for without Him this book would be pointless.

I thank Mandie for her patience and love.

I am so grateful to Dr Roger Birkman and his wife Sue, without whom our insights into personality would be much more limited. I pray that their legacy of the Birkman Method® will continue to go on to bless many people throughout the world.

Randy Cox, a long-term friend of Dr Birkman, who understood more than most, the passion Dr Birkman had for using these insights through the Church to benefit ordinary people. Thank you for helping me to keep this book true to Dr Birkman's vision.

I am grateful for the on-going support of both Birkman International Incorporated and The Birkman Foundation, without whom this book could not have been written. Keep up the good work!

John Groves, thank you for introducing me to Jesus that late night in December 1977.

Jon and Sarah Mason, thank you for introducing me to The Birkman Method®.

For reading, commenting, encouraging and being there for me, I thank Andy Phillips, Don Smith, Carol Peel, Chris Bunt, Debbie Nurse, Pete and Fran Penberthy, Dave Devenish, John Hosier, Mike Frisby, Ian Kirby and of course Dennis and Jeanette Adams.

Enormous thanks go to Dennis Adams for his love, encouragement, support and tremendous generosity, without which this book would be just another passing thought.

A special thanks to Graham Kendrick for writing great songs.

For being an exceptional Editor, I thank Abbie Robson, for her skill insight and encouragement.

Reviews

My father, Roger Birkman, often spoke of a loving God who sprinkled his personality among us — "the Priesthood of Believers" in Martin Luther's words — that every believer is a priest, a healer. It was his hope that The Birkman Method® would help people better understand themselves and each other, making way for healing and wholeness in relationship and in community. For God is not just at work from "on high", but reveals Himself to us and through us by those who walk along with us. In the same way that The Birkman Method® illuminates a path of understanding, "Being Yourself In Jesus" helps us to walk that path in Christian fellowship. I recommend it to every church, non-profit organisation and community.

Andrea Birkman
Executive Director, The Birkman Foundation
***

My father always believed his life's work with Birkman was ideally suited to helping people in churches. As a pastor's son, it was his own personal ministry to use Birkman insights for us to see, love and appreciate one another with Christ-like eyes. Colin's book has many good ideas for faith-based applications of the Birkman Method and I am sure church leaders would benefit from the insights this approach brings.

Sharon Birkman Fink
President and CEO Birkman International, Inc.
***

This is a book that really helps you to understand yourself better. Several times I found myself saying, 'oh, that's why I act or feel like that.' There's much here to help growth into greater Christian maturity.

John Hosier. Bible Teacher. Author.

***

Simply using the Birkman Method to define behaviour without including Character would be like looking at the action of a person without understanding the motive behind the action. What good does it do to know that a person has high energy if that energy is used to damage the lives of people? Or what good does it do to know that a person takes a long time to arrive at decisions if that person ends up making decisions that are hurtful to others? I sincerely believe that Character is what moulds the soul and behaviour is how the soul is outwardly expressed. You are definitely on to something. Dr Birkman would be so pleased that you are fighting the good fight.

Randy Cox Senior Birkman Consultant.
Director of Leadership Development
University Baptist Church

***

Jesus knew how to make team; by choosing different personalities in his disciples to make the gospel known to the world. These disciples did not always get on; nor do you and your church always get on! Sometimes it is sin. Sometimes we are just different – time to learn about celebrating all our differences – read this informative book, learn the principles within and then apply them to your life and church!

This book will help you understand that people are very different; a celebration of God's creative diversity and a problem to be embraced and understood if we are to enjoy being One!

Psalm 139 says we are created by God but we are not all created the same – this book helps you understand the differences God made.

We have been so helped by Colin and the principles in this book as a church; I am so thrilled this is now in written form so the Christian world can be helped!

Church Leader – ignore personality differences at your peril! We are one, but not all the same! Thank you Colin Shewry and the Birkman Method for helping us see these differences.

Andy Phillips, MTh in Applied Theology
Pastor – Open Door Church, Sunbury
***

"The first thing I thought was, 'that this seemed quite a lot of work to understand it'. I then thought, 'do I need to understand this?'. I then thought about all the pastors I know and wondered if they would benefit from this? And the answer is yes, they would really benefit from being able to gain insight into the different perspectives of the people that God gives them responsibility for".

Don Smith, Pastor.

***

This book is a very useful tool in helping us better understand ourselves and how God has made each of us with unique qualities. Furthermore, it encourages us to better understand each other and how we can relate together as God's church. It helps us explore how we can become more like Jesus, as we consider not only ourselves but how we work together with others.

In doing this we are able to better honour and value one another and see our differences as potentially complementary rather than problematic. Realising that not everyone thinks and acts like us and seeking to understand each-others uniqueness, enables us to consider how we can encourage and support one another rather than dismiss or judge each other.

This book provides a model that helps us honestly consider these things. As with any model it has limitations but nevertheless provides extremely useful insights to the whole subject.

As God's body, we are called to demonstrate His 'multifaceted nature' to the world. This book helps us grapple with some of the issues that can help or hinder this.

After many years of pastoral ministry, we feel that such a book as this deserves real consideration especially by leaders and leadership teams. It's values and insights would have helped us especially in the early years of our journey.

John & Carol Peel

***

Being Yourself in Jesus" is a fascinating and insightful way of looking at your character and personality. It's a great mix of Biblical truth and psychological analysis! I'm sure that every Christian and specifically Pastors would find this very helpful.

Jeremy Simpkins,
Christ Central Churches

***

Preface

Being Yourself in Jesus

In 1976, Graham Kendrick penned a song called "Being myself in Jesus" on his album, "Breaking of the Dawn". This spoke to me as a new Christian and today I find it still speaks. The chorus goes like this:-

> *So I'm being myself in Jesus and He's being Himself in me,*
> *I'm being myself in Jesus and that's the way to be,*
> *I'm being myself in Jesus and He's being Himself in me,*
> *And the life that He gives, is the life that I live and I'm living it naturally.*
>
> *Reproduced under licence from Graham Kendrick © 1976 Make Way Music.*
> *(Full song lyrics in appendix 1)*

But what does it mean to be 'Being myself'?

How can we understand and accept the 'me' that God made?

How can we, as mortal people deformed by sin, actually change our behaviour to be like Christ?

How do we approach this biggest of Christian struggles - how to be ourselves and yet to become more like Jesus? What should I accept and what should I change?

Many people I meet work hard at trying to change the wrong part
of themselves
and then have no energy left to change that part that
needs to change

The Old Testament shows us that we cannot successfully change ourselves through our own efforts alone. It was the same with keeping the Law where God's people tried and failed to keep it. The Law reveals sin to us but does not help us at all. Only by God's grace can we hope to be changed, to be like Jesus. As Paul said in his second letter to the Corinthians,

'Now the one who has fashioned us for this very purpose is God, who has given us the Spirit as a deposit, guaranteeing what is to come.

2 Corinthians. 5 v5

The answer is simple: it is God's grace, won for us through Jesus' death on the cross and guaranteed by the deposit of the Holy Spirit within us.

Simple……..   So why is changing such hard work?

Authors Note:

Throughout this book you may need to make notes about yourself, reminders, thoughts for later and your responses to certain exercises, so I recommend you find a note book to keep with this book, or at least make notes on the blank pages at the back.

Introduction

You are a unique individual

"Before I formed you in the womb I knew you and before you were born I consecrated you."

Jeremiah. 1 v5

God loves you, the person that He made in the womb. He loves you so much, that Jesus, God's only Son, being both fully God and fully human, died on the cross to pay the price for your sin. He defeated death and rose again. If you say yes to Him when He calls, then you are saved into a new life of following Jesus. Hallelujah!

God made you a unique individual, with an individual body and an individual personality. Together they can be seen in your behaviour. As a baby you are already unique. No two babies are alike. Even the most identical of twins know that they are different from one another.

As you grow, you then develop your own set of beliefs, values and attitudes, which add character to your body and personality. They colour and shape your behaviour. We see the results of this growth, as you develop your individual character.

These things make you, you.

A unique, individual, person!

|

The word 'character' is generally described in dictionaries as 'The mental and moral qualities distinctive to an individual.' But this definition of character as 'mental qualities', does not distinguish between the elements that are made and the elements that are learnt. Neither does 'moral qualities' account for the dynamic nature of the impact of sin and what can be learned of God's grace as the result of salvation.

Therefore, in order to better understand the unique person that you are and to then help you to focus your efforts for change in the right place, let's assume that an individual is made up of: -

Body	The physical you with its natural drives.
Personality	The mental elements that God made in you.
Character	The beliefs, values and attitudes that you learn.
Spirit	The indescribable you, which once saved, communes with God's Holy Spirit.

Throughout this book we will use the word Character to mean beliefs, values and attitudes, because when we express those attributes, the behaviour other people see is summarised by them as your Character.

Behaviour is shaped by both Body and Personality, and then further shaped by Character. As you grow and learn from all around you, you then add to your mind, experiences; knowledge, beliefs, values and attitudes. You may learn correct and helpful things or you may learn incorrect, unhelpful or even damaging things.

Your understanding changes with new information and experiences. As your beliefs, values and attitudes grow, they can sometimes lead you to make the most of your Personality but quite often they lead you away from the Personality that God made. Scripture is clear that God loves you. It is also clear that *you* should love you. Accepting and embracing the body and the Personality that God gave you in your mother's womb is His will for your life. He wove your genes into a unique blend - accept and embrace the uniqueness that He created.

My work is taken up with people who have learned to ignore their Personality in the pursuit of what others believe is best for them. "Be like your mother"; "Follow in the family business"; "You would make a great teacher, architect, priest" or "Be like your hero."

People mean well, but often their recommendations are wrong. Even a recommendation such as "Be like Christ" can be misinterpreted; it certainly does not mean 'Be a carpenter using first century methods and tools'. When Jesus said in Matthew 5 v48 "Be perfect, therefore, as your heavenly Father is perfect", I do not believe He meant that our bodies should be perfect, nor that our personalities can perfectly love our enemies. Instead, we should love in the same way the Father loves - and yet we can only do that when Jesus is in us by His Spirit; in our Character and with our Spirit.

Unique yet conforming to the image of Christ

I believe that people are happiest and most productive when they understand, accept and embrace their unique Personality. Most psychologists and business coaches would agree with such a statement, although they might add 'effective behaviours' that 'can' make you more or less successful. However, these leadership qualities or 'effective management behaviours' often do not take account of the underlying Personality and may even ride roughshod over them. More importantly they may not recommend that people should shape their Character to be like Christ.

For example, my friend Geoff has been made by God to **Need** competition in his life. However, somewhere in his upbringing he has learnt that competition is bad. Rather, he should be humble and collaborative, a team player and he should always put others first. He must not be individually competitive, 'it's not cricket you know' (meaning it is not socially acceptable). Consequently, now as a more mature adult, he is not seen as competitive, because he learnt not to behave that way. Yet internally the Need to compete leaves him terribly frustrated and worse still, if you pay him a complement, it feels like a win, so he then feels terrible because that contradicts his deeply held belief about himself that it is wrong to win. If he doesn't win, he is frustrated by the God-given Need to win. If he does win he is frustrated by his deeply held belief that it is wrong to win. This has created an internal tension within him which is a very damaging lose/lose situation that has had a very negative impact on his life. This tension exists within His Personality, but with Christ in him, his Character can overcome this tension.

God loves the unique person that you are. He wants you to love the person that you are too. You cannot change the Personality God gave you, but you *can* change your beliefs, values and attitudes, even though they can be quite ingrained and hard to shift. God wants to sanctify and purify your Character in order to be like Christ.

The message at the very heart of this book is this: -

Be the Personality that God made you to be, with a Character that is like Christ's.

This book tells you how.

1

What it is to be a Human?

For you created my inmost being; you knit me together in my mother's womb. I praise you because I am fearfully and wonderfully made; your works are wonderful, I know that full well. My frame was not hidden from you when I was made in the secret place, when I was woven together in the depths of the earth. Your eyes saw my unformed body; all the days ordained for me were written in your book before one of them came to be. How precious to me are your thoughts, God! How vast is the sum of them! Were I to count them, they would outnumber the grains of sand. When I awake, I am still with you.

Psalm. 139 v13-18

Last year I was helping a church leadership team to understand how each of them is unique and brings different Strengths to the team, and, more importantly, helping them to value one another and engage with the differences between them.

Nigel, one of the leaders, asked if he could ask a question. "Of course" I replied. He struggled to find the words to ask, "Is it ok to be me and also do this job? I think people want to have someone more like their expectations of a church leader". Nigel is very direct and to the point and not a very 'pastoral' personality. He felt people expected lots of sympathy and listening whereas his skill was to see through the issues and make clear recommendations. Because of this, he wondered if he should no longer be one of the leaders of the church.

And yet, before I even started to answer his question, the others in their leadership team jumped in with "No, no you're wrong, we love it when you 'do a Nigel!' When we are struggling to come to a conclusion, you arrive and say 'these are the options and I think you should do this one.' It is so helpful to have that skill as part of the team, otherwise we might just ramble-on and never make any decisions."

Out of my distant memory popped a Graham Kendrick song which I hadn't heard since the late 1970s: -

> *Being myself is not half so bad as I thought that it might be.*
> *Living in the love of Jesus, who loves the likes of me*
> *And isn't it good to know, I don't even have to try*
> *To fight for a place in this old human race, since I'm already home and dry.*

> *So I'm being myself in Jesus and He's being Himself in me.*
> *I'm being myself in Jesus and that's the way to be.*
> *I'm being myself in Jesus and He's being Himself in me*
> *And the life that He gives is the life that I live and I'm living it naturally.*
>
> *Graham Kendrick © 1976 Make Way Music.*

Nigel did not need to change his Personality to be like either his, or the church's, idea of a leader, rather he needed to be the leader God had made him to be, being himself in Jesus. By becoming aware of each individual's unique contribution and how each Personality complements the others, the leadership team were given the opportunity to become even more effective than they already were.

Of course, simply being yourself in Jesus is not a passive thing; it's not just hanging out and doing whatever you want. First you have to understand yourself, in which way God uniquely made your Personality and how that Personality can effectively work with others. Only then can you understand how Jesus can be Himself in you and allow the Holy Spirit to be in you throughout every day, informing every decision and shaping how you behave towards other people.

We will look at humans through a number of different perspectives in order to understand this concept. Of course, you cannot in reality, break a human into their constituent parts to see what's there, but looking at ourselves from some key perspectives helps us make sense of what 'being yourself' looks like, as well as learning how to let Jesus be Himself.

First Things First

In this book, we're aiming to help you better understand yourself and how other people are different from you, sometimes very different. In discovering how to understand ourselves better, it is important to start by understanding God Himself. However, there are plenty of books, not least the Bible, which can help us focus on God's nature. One element of understanding comes from the truth that God makes us like Himself.

God said,

> *'Let us make mankind in our image, in our likeness, so that they may rule over the fish in the sea and the birds in the sky, over the livestock and all the wild animals and over all the creatures that move along the ground.'*

So God created mankind in His own image, in the image of God He created them; male and female He created them.

God blessed them and said to them, 'Be fruitful and increase in number; fill the earth and subdue it. Rule over the fish in the sea and the birds in the sky and over every living creature that moves on the ground."

Genesis. 1 v26-28

Whilst we are physical creatures like other animals, we are primarily spiritual beings like God is Himself. Once saved, our spirit is re-born and we become co-heirs with Christ just as Paul said,

'For those who are led by the Spirit of God are the children of God. The Spirit you received does not make you slaves, so that you live in fear again; rather, the Spirit you received brought about your adoption to sonship. And by him we cry, 'Abba, Father.' The Spirit himself testifies with our spirit that we are God's children. Now if we are children, then we are heirs – heirs of God and co-heirs with Christ, if indeed we share in his sufferings in order that we may also share in his glory.'

Romans. 8 v14-16

It is therefore important, as we explore being human through a number of different perspectives, that we don't lose sight of the fact we are spiritual beings. It is our spiritual nature that enables us to commune with God and Him with us. However, in starting to explore who we are, we need to push our physical and spiritual nature into the background for a moment and first look at ourselves as *human* beings, with a Personality and a Character.

Personality (or... The Unchanging You)

Most psychologists do not attempt to separate Personality and Character, generally pouring all of their ideas in to one mix called 'the person'. But I have found that it's helpful to separate them in our thinking, because, as Christians, if we can differentiate between the Personality that God has given and the Character which has developed as we learn and grow, then we can be much clearer about what needs to change.

God gave each of us a unique Personality; it is what we are born with, as He said through the Psalmist,

> *'Know that the Lord is God. It is he who made us, and we are his;*
> *we are his people, the sheep of his pasture.'*
>
> Psalm. 100 v3

And, if God gives us our Personality, then our Personality is a good thing, as we see in James,

> *Every good and perfect gift is from above, coming down from the Father of the heavenly lights, who does not change like shifting shadows. He chose to give us birth through the word of truth, that we might be a kind of first-fruits of all he created.*
>
> James. 1v17

Personality is a God-given gift

Personality is more complex than the basic needs of breathing or eating. Personality is a fixed and unchangeable set of aspects, which drive us, or motivate us, affecting the way we behave. These measurable Personality elements are strong, clear and persistently the same over time.

For example, you might be designed with a need to make decisions quickly or slowly. Neither is right or wrong but simply different. You may be decisive or reflective. Perhaps energetic or have a need to conserve energy. It could be that you may love talking with others and being part of the group or then you might be more comfortable alone or with just one or two close friends. None of these are wrong, they are simply different. These Personality traits are in you from birth.

A measure of Personality

Dr Roger Birkman, the son of a Lutheran Pastor, served the Allied Cause in WW2 as a B-17 Pilot in the US 8th Army Air Corps. Before the war, he had been intrigued by the different perceptions implied by the 'speck and a log' that Jesus described in the 'Sermon on the Mount'. This interest in perspectives grew during his war experience, as he repeatedly observed that his crew members were reporting identical events in strikingly different ways, sometimes directly contradicting each other during the de-briefing after each sortie. He realised that each person had a unique perspective that coloured what was seen and how it was reported. It was this curiosity into the significance of each person's perceptions that became the springboard for The Birkman Method®.

Roger's B-17 was shot down shortly before D-Day (all his crew survived the war) and he was hidden by the Belgian Underground for three months until he was liberated in early September, 1944. In that same period, Margaret 'Sue' Leath worked for Humble Oil with Roger's cousins and she had been praying, along with them, for his safe return. When those prayers were answered, a celebration picnic was held in Houston's Hermann Park. It was at that picnic that Roger and Sue met. She joined Roger on the 'mission' and they were married in 1945 at First Methodist Church in Houston, where they remained very active members. Sue continued working so that Roger could pursue his degrees. He went on to earn his PhD in Psychology with a thesis titled 'The Test of Social Comprehension' that later became The Birkman Method®.

At first, Dr Birkman was a voice crying in the wilderness, as most of psychology at that time was focused on abnormal behaviour, but Roger had chosen to explore the psychology of normal behaviour instead. In 1951, Birkman & Associates, the precursor of Birkman International, was formed, with Sue as the first associate. She hand-scored each person's responses, a lengthy and laborious task, where only two or three reports could be completed in a day.

Later, Dr Birkman saw that computers had the potential to expedite the entire process and grow the amount of empirical data much more quickly. However, many psychologists were appalled that he dared to use computers and 'reduce people to a set of numbers'.

But Roger and Sue shared a different vision — they knew that computers were just a tool to help understand perceptions. Together they pressed on with what they saw as their God-given mission: to help people gain insight into how their own perceptions colour everything they do. After enduring many tests of faith, Dr Birkman, his insights and his methods were finally vindicated. The success of The Birkman Method® allowed him to establish both the 'Ministry Reports' system for the faith communities and 'The Birkman Foundation' in the non-profit arena.

Today the Birkman Method® is considered by many to be the best personality assessment in the world.

However, I want you to understand that this is not another worldly set of ideas which I am trying to put upon the Church; rather it is a helpful approach that agrees with and complements scripture. In fact it is helpful to anyone, in business or not. The Birkman Method® is used by businesses, charities and churches, in leadership development, marriage workshops, retirement planning, worship groups, - in fact it has been used in nearly every ministry area of service, as well as with some of the largest business organisations in the world.

Character (or... The 'You', You Have Learned to Be?)

Character is learnt. It is the set of beliefs, values and attitudes that we hold, as individuals, the consequences of which are expressed in the way we behave. People, who then observe that behaviour, attribute those beliefs, values and attitudes to our Character. However, unlike Personality, we choose these traits as we grow. We do not enter the world with our Character fully formed - we learn from parents, siblings, friends, teachers, authors, media and other people that we hold in high regard. This is the part of our complete persona, which is constantly changing as we take on new knowledge, ideas and experiences.

Character is learnt

Some knowledge and ideas persist and you see them as being important or strong, they therefore become your beliefs that can be quite solid in your thinking and hard to change. Some beliefs become so important to you that they become your values. These can be very hard to change indeed, even if they are wrong beliefs.

And yet Character is malleable. A deeply held value or belief is very difficult to shift and sometimes seems impossible to change, which is why our history is peppered with martyrs who refused to sacrifice their belief, even to death. Character can be shaped, we can change. We know that people can be persuaded to change their view and in some circumstances, other people can cause us to behave in the most remarkable ways, for either good or evil.

This way of thinking, separating Personality and Character, does need some effort to come to grips with. Some people ask me if it is reasonable to equate knowledge, experience and even wisdom with Character. The answer I believe is yes. The few reflexes we are born with are a tiny amount of our adult knowledge. It is knowledge that we choose to believe or disbelieve and it's our experiences that reinforce what we learn. If I learn a particular subject to a great depth and have considerable experience in a subject and learn how to effectively apply that knowledge, then people might consider that I have some wisdom in that area.

Here's an example: if you got to know me, you would learn about the things I believe are important and true by interacting with me.

Through conversation and observation of me, you would make judgements about my Character: - Am I nice? Am I kind? Am I compassionate? Am I knowledgeable? Or am I cruel? Dismissive of others? Unkind? or ignorant? These behaviours do not come from my God-given Personality, but have been learnt as I have grown. You would also learn that I have a great depth of knowledge and skill in applying that knowledge, when it comes to helping people understand their Personality. Therefore, you would consider that I have a degree of wisdom in that subject.

God of course also gives wisdom as a gift and there are many times I have not had an answer, but I have asked for wisdom and God has generously answered with Godly wisdom. All these learnt areas I refer to as Character, because they are different from the Personality that I was born with. There may be some who argue that Character is about a moral position or ethical issues. It is my view, that our values are formed from our beliefs and beliefs are based on our knowledge. Some people reading this will see a concrete difference between different categories of knowledge. However, in my experience I've found it very hard to find any knowledge in the world that does not have an ethical edge to it somewhere.

Therefore, I prefer the simple and pragmatic view that all knowledge forms the basis of our beliefs, values and attitudes and consequently it is reasonable to represent these things as separate from our God-given Personality. The word that I feel fits the best, is Character. We are born with a Personality, given to us by God through our genes and then we develop a Character based on what we believe as we grow.

Why separate Personality and Character?

I have met many people who believe that they should be trying to change their Personality, trying to be more extroverted or less extroverted. They may think they should be more structured or less structured, more direct or more diplomatic, more team-minded or more individually competitive, too busy or not busy enough.

Each of the above are Personality traits, so in each of these cases, they are trying to change their unique Personality, rather than being the person that God made them to be.

I always tell them that God may not help them change that part of themselves. Why should He if He made you that way?

God may not help you change your Personality.

Why should He?

He made you that way.

However, if you have developed a selfish or dishonest Character, are comfortable with lies and manipulation, or have no hesitation in betraying someone else for your own selfish gain, then He definitely wants you to change these Character issues and He will help you to change. That is why it is worth the effort of separating Personality from Character. It is the centre of this book so that you can clearly see what needs to change and what doesn't.

By separating the two elements of Personality and Character, you can then stop trying to change your God-given Personality and start to put your effort and prayers into changing your Character, even adopting the Character of Christ.

The mind is the battleground of our choices

This is a Christian book and therefore you might reasonably ask about the impact of the 'flesh' (as Paul described it) and of sin, on our Personality and Character.

Paul, when referring to the 'flesh' did not mean the body, which has had some bad press over the years and is seen by many as the source of most of our problems.

People have tried many approaches for disciplining the body and keeping it in check. Some have tried to 'deny the flesh' through excessive fasting and even punished 'the flesh' through flagellation in an attempt at gaining holiness. Such techniques always fail, because in blaming the body they miss the key issue. Babies do not have a problem with the body, but as children grow, they may learn very unhelpful ways of caring for their physical nature. I believe we have to start by loving ourselves. Love is the key to our bodies, our Personality and our Character. The battle is not with our bodies. The battle is in our mind.

Paul, when referring to 'the flesh', did mean the impact of sin that is in us from birth. Sin is a tricky thing to understand. Hundreds of books have been dedicated to this very complex subject. Before we explore the impact of sin on our Personality and Character, we need to understand ourselves better by learning more about how these elements work. Only then can we understand more easily the impact of sin.

Imagine teaching a child to draw a tree. We will probably tell them that drawing a brown stick with a green squiggle on top, is a fabulous tree! As adults we know that this is not true, but it gives the child the first bit of understanding to build on. It takes many years to get to understand the multitude of nuances that can be found in the world of trees, but we have to start somewhere. This book, like the stick drawing, will increase in complexity with each chapter, as we add layers of complexity to our understanding of the whole person.

When you get to the place where you can understand and value your unchanging Personality, and then recognise that your Character is your choice and is changeable, only then you can consider the impact of sin on your whole persona.

Christ paid the penalty for sin once and for all, but the everyday battle to overcome the consequences of sin, our sinful nature, is not in our Personality, it is in our beliefs and choices – that is, our Character. Your Character is your battleground, not your physical body and not your Personality. This is why we need to understand Personality and Character first and then look at the impact of sin.

A summary of the order of understanding: -

- In order to be yourself; you must first accept, value and honour your body and its reasonable needs.

- Then you must understand, accept, value and embrace the Personality God gave you through your genes when you were made in the womb.

- Having accepted your Personality, you need to search and know (Psalm.139 v23) your Character, because it is here that the battle with sin takes place.

- With the help of the Holy Spirit, your Character can overcome your sinful nature when it appears in that battle within your mind.

- We do not have perfect insight. Understanding a little is like seeing through a glass darkly or a reflection in a poor mirror (1 Corinthians. 13 v12). It does help us to focus our prayers and effort into changing those parts of ourselves that can and should be changed, in order to be more like Christ and produce the fruit of the Holy Spirit.

2

The Greatest Commandment

Understanding and appreciating our Personality and Character, while a really beneficial thing to do, is not an end in itself. The reason we need to understand this subject, is that it really helps us to achieve the most important commandments that Jesus gives us.

'Hearing that Jesus had silenced the Sadducees, the Pharisees got together. One of them, an expert in the law, tested him with this question: 'Teacher, which is the greatest commandment in the Law?'

Jesus replied: "'Love the Lord your God with all your heart and with all your soul and with all your mind." This is the first and greatest commandment. And the second is like it: "Love your neighbour as yourself." All the Law and the Prophets hang on these two commandments.'

Matthew. 22 v34-40

In this passage, Jesus was replying to a question from experts in the Law who were hoping to catch Him out. So Jesus answers with a statement that fulfils the Law and then goes much further than the Law did itself. The Law given to Moses included such things as; 'You shall have no other Gods before me, you shall not bow to an image of a God, love Me and keep my commandments'.

However, Jesus is saying 'Love with all your heart and with all your soul and with all your mind', in other words, love God with every part of your life. Jesus' commandment is bigger than the Law, He commands us to love in a greater way than was commanded of Moses.

Commanding someone to 'love' might sound strange, but this is because we need to understand the context of the words Jesus used. In the West we have romanticised the word 'love' as something we fall uncontrollably into, or something we really, really like. Jesus was using the word love, to mean a sacrificial love; we must love God with every part of us and in everything we do.

He used the word 'command' because the Pharisees would understand this from the perspective of the Law. To understand how we, who receive God's grace freely, can also obey a commandment to love is essential. The commands to love God and to love our neighbour as ourselves are unchangeable. However, the response is different for the unsaved and the saved.

The unsaved person can only respond to the command to love from within the law in which they live. The Pharisee might work hard to love God through obedience to every aspect of the Law, but we know that no matter how hard such a person tries, they will fail. The Law offers nothing to help the unsaved person, so they are on their own with the struggle of keeping the Law. This is the reason that God sent His only Son, to change the relationship with mankind for evermore.

The saved person responds from God's grace, the command is the same, but now it comes from within a different relationship. Now I act because I want to please and obey my Lord, because I am adopted into His family and I am a co-heir with Christ. More importantly I have the Holy Spirit within me to empower me to respond to the command. Here I am commanded to obey, but with such love and grace this command hardly feels like a command at all.

For he chose us in him before the creation of the world to be holy and blameless in his sight. In love he predestined us for adoption to sonship through Jesus Christ, in accordance with his pleasure and will to the praise of his glorious grace, which he has freely given us in the One he loves.

Ephesians. 1 v5

As adopted children, we cannot help but love our Heavenly Father. We will want to honour and bless Him as part of that love and so we seek out what He desires. He does not simply want the duty, service or obedience of a slave, the angels do that already. No, He wants relationship with us and for us to love Him with all our heart, with all our soul and with all our mind. When we love God in such a way, then we of course want to serve Him and be obedient to His ways. As Paul said, "I am a servant to Christ." (Romans. 1 v1), but it is the servanthood of a son or daughter and not that of a slave to the Law.

Understanding this is critical if you want to change. We can easily fall back into behaving as a slave to law, rather than embracing the freedom that comes in the gospel of grace that God gives.

If you read this book and respond to it as a formula, as if it were a law, then you will not achieve the change you may hope for, because you will remain a slave to the Law. However, if you read this book and respond to it as helpful encouragement from God, who has placed a seed in you at salvation to grow through your life and He will be with you by His Spirit to help you change, then you will achieve much more than you can hope for.

So when we understand this and accept Him as Lord we receive the Holy Spirit, 'the seed of Christ' (1 John. 3 v9) in us that steadily grows, then we cannot help but to love our Father with all our heart and all our soul and our entire mind. This 'commandment' is simply stating the obvious, that as a son or daughter we cannot help but love Him.

Second Commandment

How can we love ourselves if we do not know ourselves?

The reason I have been emphasising this first commandment so much, is because if we can understand something of the enormity of the 'Greatest Commandment', then we can also understand something of the second commandment which Jesus said is like the first, "Love your neighbour as yourself".

While this is clearly a statement by Jesus about how we should behave towards our neighbours, which is everybody, it also speaks about how we should love ourselves.

As someone once said, "I pity your neighbour, because I have seen how terrible you are at loving yourself!"

If we do not know how to love ourselves well, then how can we know how to love our neighbour well? How can we love ourselves if we do not know ourselves?

When we have a clear view of the truth about ourselves and are able to accept and embrace who God made us to be, we can also gain a much clearer view of others. It then becomes much easier to value, honour and love others with a love that reveals God's love that is the heart of the gospel.

As Jesus said,

> '*A new command I give you: love one another. As I have loved you, so you must love one another. By this everyone will know that you are my disciples, if you love one another.*'
>
> John. 13 v24-35

In loving ourselves, we are not talking about selfishness; we are talking about an honest 'God view' of ourselves. A view where we can honour and thank God for ourselves, be kind to ourselves, ensure that we respect and value the person God made us to be, to choose to act in ways that help keep us healthy in mind and body.

This is the basis for making the effort to understand and embrace our Personality and then to choose to believe and adopt the Character of Christ.

Truth is releasing

One of the most important things in being a Christian is actually valuing who God made you to be. If you do not have an honest view of yourself, then it is hard to be honest with other people. If you don't understand your own unique Personality, then you will not understand just how much other people are different from you. Being different from each other is no accident, it is the way God designed us to be.

Let me explain with an example. I met with Paul and John, two leaders from a medium sized UK Church. They were about to undertake some changes in the administration team and wanted to see if I could help. Both of them were quite direct and to the point in their communication style, they never held back but launched straight into the matter at hand. It was clear the two got on well together and there was some vigorous discussion.

However, whilst that aspect of their Personality was similar, there were other aspects that weren't. They both talked with the same 'to the point' style, but whilst John needed that same direct approach from other people, Paul needed a much more sensitive and diplomatic style from the people around him, if he was to avoid feeling hurt by other people's directness - especially from people who were important to him. This difference was invisible in the discussions they had with one another, but while Paul knew that he could easily be hurt if people were too direct with him, he hid it away and was almost embarrassed by this part of himself.

I asked if I could reveal some of the differences that I could see from the personality assessments I'd undertaken with them, to which they both agreed. While there were many differences, I already knew which was likely to be a crucial issue, so I turned to John and said: -

"John, in your conversations, you are very direct and to the point and you are comfortable with having a robust discussion with Paul. Is this correct?" "Yes" was the reply.

"And of course you are very happy when Paul is direct or even blunt with you?" "Yes of course" he replied.

"And Paul you are very happy to be direct and almost blunt with John?" Paul replied positively.

"But Paul, I bet that John doesn't know, that when he is blunt with you, it can actually hurt you and if it does, you have to suppress and hide that pain?"

I had hit the point and there was an extended silence while Paul struggled to know what to say.

As I explained to these two lovely men, our needs are often hidden away, and while we behave in what we feel is the best way we can, one person's bluntness can still be damaging to another person who finds such directness difficult. Only by knowing ourselves well and appreciating how others are different from us, do we get to the point where we can be open with each other.

Following this meeting, John and Paul continue to have robust discussion, but John is much more aware that this can cause Paul discomfort so they have agreed that John tries to be a bit more sensitive with Paul. Paul speaks out if he is feeling uncomfortable, knowing that John's response will be one of love and acceptance. This small change grew their mutual trust, love and honour.

She goes on and on and he's not listening!

One couple in our Church had always struggled with their communication with each other. Nothing new in that! However, through one of our courses they discovered one important area of difference between them, which enabled them to articulate the problem and develop a new strategy, making communication much better.   Sarah needed to tell all the details of a story in a linear style, always starting right from the beginning. However, Jonathan only wanted to know the important bits and not go over the whole story again. In fact he found it embarrassing having to listen to the whole story again when Sarah retold it to other people.

The course had opened the issue for them and as they explored their differences they were able to articulate the problems with each other in such a way that they found a strategy that both enabled Sarah to re-tell the whole story and enabled Jonathan to only listen to the new or relevant bits.

Now when Sarah starts a story, she tries to tell Jonathan the important bits first and then works her way through the story from beginning to end. Jonathan pays close attention to the important bits at the beginning and nods politely through the rest while getting on with other things. They are both very happy with this arrangement and this has resolved much of their communication tensions.

The key to these relationship improvements is in understanding how God made us unique and appreciating that other people are different from us. In this way we value and appreciate difference and even learn how the differences complement each-other. Therefore, there is no need to judge or criticise the differences in God-given personalities, instead we can celebrate the richness of God's creativity.

It's not magic, it's how we are made

As well as appreciating the differences between us, we can also predict some behaviour from knowing just a little. For example, people who love a clear and detailed plan, will probably also enjoy numbers and number puzzles and will probably avoid holidays where there is lots of novelty with foods and drinks that are very different from what they are used to. Likewise, people who love to talk and persuade others might find numbers dry and draining. Similarly, people who love being outdoors, might be quite indifferent to art and music whilst art-lovers may not value being outdoors.

This isn't always the case though. For example, people who know me, know that I love music and am reasonably musical, I love playing bass guitar and am happy to spend money on a good set of headphones. I also love art and the aesthetic quality of things - in recent years I have learnt to paint watercolours. However, a trait that often goes alongside music and art, is a love of words and literature. Whilst that is true of most people who are musical and artistic, it is not true of me as an individual. Words are something I struggle with and find draining.

Dr Birkman found through extensive study that it was possible to predict that if we like one thing, then we probably like a set of other things, but this would not be true for every measurement for an individual. We are all truly unique.

Once you recognise that the Personality differences are God given, you can then start to understand your own uniqueness and celebrate the differences between you and the people around you. Then you can accommodate the differences more easily and build more effective relationships with others, be that with individuals or groups.

By recognising, valuing and embracing our God-given Personality and the unique personalities God has given to others, we are much better placed to love God with all our Heart and our Mind and our Soul.

We are then also in a better place to love ourselves.

Focus points for the Greatest Commandment: -

- Love God first, love yourself second and then you will find it easier to love your neighbour.

- Always remember the mess from which God saved you, it helps you stay humble. Then remember what Jesus has done for you so you can celebrate the truth.

- God created the person that you are, celebrate His creation! The past has gone, the future is with Him and you are renewed in your mind one step at a time for His glory.

- God did not ignore the Law, rather through a clear process; His Son Jesus Christ fulfilled the Law and then exceeded the Law through His love and grace. So now you can obey His command to love by the power of His grace.

- God's action in sending His Son to die on the Cross was outrageous. Having won you on the cross He now leads you gently to grow in love a little at a time.

3

The Map, a shorthand of helpful colours

Jesus wanted to teach His disciples, so He used stories. He knew that using parables were an effective way of getting His disciples to think about His underlying message; while at the same time being easy to grasp and remember. Jesus disciples asked why He spoke in parables and amongst the reasons He gave, He said: -

> *"But blessed are your eyes because they see, and your ears because they hear. For truly I tell you, many prophets and righteous people longed to see what you see but did not see it, and to hear what you hear but did not hear it. Listen then to what the parable of the sower means: "*

Matthew. 13 v16-17

Jesus then went on to help the disciples to understand the parable.

We all know that people are very complex and therefore explaining Personality is also complicated. Dr Birkman recognised that describing Personality could be very hard to apply if there was not some easy way, like a parable, to remember and use the insights, so he developed a map of four colours. The map, like Jesus's stories, are designed to be thought provoking, tangible and an easy way to remember the insights that Dr Birkman has provided us with.

Printing in colour is a very difficult task, which we have not attempted for this book. However, you will see on the back cover a square divided into four coloured quadrants: Red, Green, Blue and Yellow.

This is Dr Birkman's map. This is an important tool that we will use continuously as we go through this book together. The colours and their meanings and position relative to each other are all very important.

When you look at the image on the back cover, you will notice the four colours are arranged into four quadrants divided by two central lines, one vertical and one horizontal. This can be thought of as a map of all the different Personality types in the world. Your unique Personality map will be made up of three different perspectives, which will form a triangle shape on the map and with over 940 billion possible triangles; your triangle is truly unique. The image shows the four key colours of the map which you need to learn.

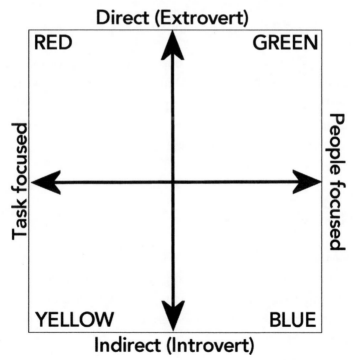

The Birkman Method®

Throughout the rest of the book we will use the above map to explain the layout, colours and meanings.

The map is formed around two dimensions, 'extrovert against introvert', and, 'task focused or people focused'. These are described with a score ranging from 0-99. Scores that are at the extremes of 0 or 99 are the most intense but with opposite meanings, where a score of 50 is a balance of both extremes.

The vertical arrow shows that people who are towards the top of the map are more direct or extrovert in what they say and do. A high score, which would be at the edge of the map, would be very extrovert. People at the bottom of the map tend to be less direct and more subtle and introverted.

A very low score at the bottom edge would be very introverted.

The horizontal arrow shows that people to the left of the map tend to focus on the tasks at hand before thinking about the people, whereas the people on the right will tend to put people first and think about the task later. Again, a low or high score would be close to the edge of the map and show a stronger intensity.

Some hard work required

The four colours of the Birkman Map® are something we will refer to, many times within this book and you will find it incredibly helpful, both in learning about yourself and how others are different from you. It does however, take effort to learn and remember, but it is really worth that effort.

Learning the map will help you throughout your life

Dr Birkman gave each corner of the map a different colour.

      Red   = Direct (Extrovert) and Task focused.
      Green   = Direct (Extrovert) and People focused.
      Blue   = Indirect (Introvert) and People focused.
      Yellow = Indirect (Introvert) and Task focused.

Draw your own map now, like the one above, and label it extrovert at the top, introvert at the bottom, task focused on the left and people focused on the right. Then add each of the four colours into their correct quadrant. Drawing it yourself helps to embed this into your thinking.

How briefly can it be said?

The following four statements are worth remembering as they will always help you remember the more detailed descriptions we will talk through. It will help you to make a note of the following four statements, so on the map you have drawn, add the text in to each quarter

      Red   =   Doer
      Green   =   Communicator
      Blue   =   Thinker
      Yellow =   Analyser

Saying it again, but with some detail

The four quadrants have the same meanings throughout this book, so let me explain them with just a little more detail. You will find that you will come back to these descriptions a number of times so make a note of the page number in your notebook.

Red - Doer - (Getting things done)

Red people tend to focus on the task and be very direct in the way they address people and tasks. You may see them as rather an extrovert or outspoken.

Red people are friendly, logical and energetic who tend to call a spade a spade. They tell you what they think and want to get to the point, make things work and understand what is practical and tangible. They tend to live and thrive in the moment - people in the extreme corner will probably associate themselves with a slogan such as "Just do it".

Green - Communicator - (Interacting with and influencing people)

Green people tend to focus on people before thinking about a task but like their Red friends, they are direct and rather extroverted, so they will tell you what they think.

Green people love talking with other people and therefore love to be in the company of others (so they can talk with them). They also tend to live in the moment to see who they can talk with right now. They are inspired by novel ideas or the latest gadget, and will try to persuade you how wonderful something is. Because they are flexible you may find next week they will have something even better to persuade you about. Green people love to compete and win - people in the extreme corner really can persuade Eskimos to buy ice.

Blue - Thinker - (Being creative and strategic)

Blue people, like their Green friends, focus more on people than on the task that needs to be done, but they are much more subtle, thoughtful and introverted about how they will communicate and engage with people.

Blue people tend to be creative, insightful, thoughtful and reflective, and prefer to have just a few close but really good friends. Their optimistic nature generally considers every action in terms of what impact it may have on their own future and on that of other people.

People in the extreme corner can seem very introverted and might only ever open up to one or two close friends.

Yellow - Analyser - (Being structured and ordered)

Yellow people, like their Blue friends, are quite subtle and indirect or introverted in what they say and do, but like their Red friends, they focus on the task before thinking about the people.

Yellow people are structured, ordered and focussed on the process. They consider every action based on the evidence of what has worked before - if it works, why change it? This cautious approach leans on historic evidence because history speaks to what will work in the future. Using this information, they can concentrate and create solid logical plans and processes and they really appreciate that the rules are there for a reason. People in the extreme corner can be very introverted and can appear almost obsessive about their tasks.

Central

Some people have a Personality that is close to the middle of the map. Generally, they can understand something of each of the colours but will struggle to understand the extremes of all four colours.

Daily route-finding using the map

Now you have an understanding of what the four-colour map on the back cover means. Think about where you might put yourself on the map by picking the colour description that you relate to the most. If you have drawn your own map, add a mark where you guess you might appear on it.

Now using the four descriptions above, think about someone you know who has the same description as yourself - it is usually easy to think of such a person, as we are attracted to, and tend to make friends with, people whose Personality is like our own.

Now look at the map and think about the colour that is alongside your own. Can you think of a person you know whose Personality fits this description? Consider the differences between you. When you identify such differences, you are really identifying that you are uniquely different from that person and yet together, by bringing those differences to complement each other, you are starting to see how teamwork actually works.

Now look again at the map and think of someone who fits the description of the colour above or below your colour. Once you have thought about them, contrast them to the person whose colour is alongside yours. You may instantly realise that whilst both are different from you in some ways, they are very different from each other. This is because diagonal separation on the map shows the greatest differences in Personality.

Finally try and think of someone whose colour is diagonally opposite to you. This can be quite hard for many people, because people who are diagonal to us, sometimes fall in to the category of "I just don't understand them at all". Things that are true of one colour will have the opposite meaning for the diagonal colour, meaning that their Personality, whilst very different from you, will also be the most complementary to your own Personality.

People I do not like

I once heard a business speaker on the radio describe how he always selected key employees that he simply didn't like, as he found this created the most effective teams. He was, of course, right - but for the wrong reason. We tend to like people who are like us in terms of Personality. People with the diagonally opposed colour are the most different from us and therefore we can easily dismiss them as 'this is someone I don't like', when in truth it is someone we don't understand.

However, they will make the greatest contribution to your team because they are so different from you.

I thought I didn't like them,

but it turns out I did not understand them

If this section has made sense to you, then well done. You are now better equipped to understand the world of people around you and maybe you have discovered that those people you don't get on with, are simply different from you. Understanding that alone will change your view of them and you are on the way to understanding your uniqueness and how we are different from all the other unique people around us.

Before taking a closer look at the map, satisfy yourself that you have got the foundation we have just described clear in your mind or at least drawn your own map. This is a key step in developing your understanding.

Uniqueness and difference

One perspective we will look at is called Interests. Now by Interests we don't mean hobbies or pastimes. What we mean is that there are certain subjects, hardwired into you when you were made, that trigger your passion. For me my important Interests are, getting things fixed and understanding how things work. However, my most potent Interest is music. I can't ignore music when I stumble on it, sound in any form is important to me, as is silence.

If there were 100 jobs in front of me and if just one involved music, then I would take that one, because I am energised by sound. It is easy for me to put my energy into sound and the more I do, the more energy I find I have (until I'm exhausted and have to sleep). In contrast, my lowest Interest area, which involves organising and structuring things such as my paper-work or my CD collection, drains me dry. Just thinking about such tasks exhaust me, and therefore I hate such clerical tasks and avoid them whenever possible, God did not make me for such things.

Interests are shown on the map as an asterisk. You can see from the map below that my Interests are Red and Red people like to make things work, to fix things and to fix people. This explains in part why I am writing a book that is designed to make things better for you and your Church, by helping you to understand the world better. When I am engaged in a task or person that has a problem, you will see me as being quite extrovert and unhesitant about sticking my nose in and trying to sort it out or speak into the issue at hand.

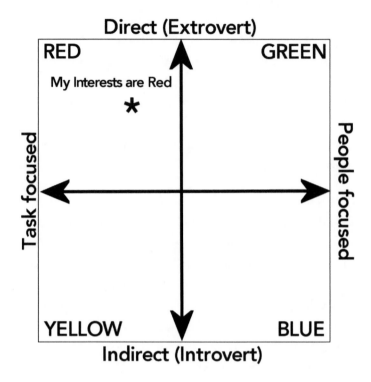

The Birkman Map®

Interests are shown on the map as an asterisk. You can see from the above map that my Interests are Red and Red people like to make things work, to fix things and to fix people. This explains in part why I am writing a book that is designed to make things better for you and your Church, by helping you to understand the world better. When I am engaged in a task or person that has a problem, you will see me as being quite extrovert and unhesitant about sticking my nose in and trying to sort it out or speak into the issue at hand.

Dr Birkman was able to group a number of Red attributes together so you might reasonably guess that all the Red interests apply to me. Life is not that simple, but some do apply. From Dr Birkman's work we know that most people who have Red Interests like me will not be likely to have Blue Interests as they are diagonally opposite Red, that is, the least like Red on the map. You can test this by asking some questions like, how important is music, or art or literature to me? (These are all typically Blue Interests.)

This is where the truth of each person's uniqueness appears. I confirm my 'Redness' when I tell you that I find words draining, I read but it is tiring and writing is hard work, typical of a Red person. However, art is quite important to me and music is essential. So now you know that I am a mix of Red and Blue, but Red is stronger so when all my Interests are added together I am Red. I will tend to look at the world with a 'Red' perspective, but you now know I am also able to understand the Blue Interest perspective as well.

Let me introduce you to Andrew. Below is a map showing his Interests.

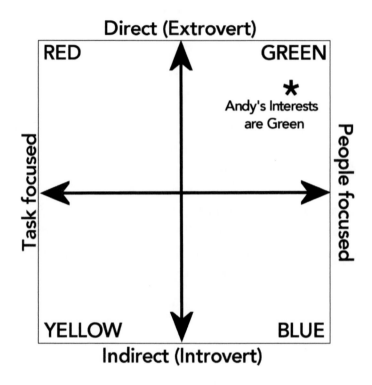

The Birkman Map®

Andy's Interests are Green. He loves talking to people, persuading them and helping them. He also loves winning, everything, at some level, is a competition. He is very loud and he loves people.

Now you have a little insight into people with Red and Green Interests.

Imagine for a moment that we are both in a car which breaks down on the side of the road.

Imagine how will Colin react?

Now imagine how Andy will react?

If you imagined me with my sleeves rolled up, with my head in the engine working through a set of things that might have gone wrong, then you are spot on.

If you imagined Andy somewhat like 'Basil Fawlty' shouting and warning the car to behave and then trying to beat the car into submission with a branch, then you might not be too far out.

In truth, I will try and fix it by getting my hands dirty and Andy will persuade someone who knows what they are doing to fix it for him. Neither approach is wrong, but different. I might have more success if I can spot the problem and Andy might have more success by persuading a mechanic to fix it.

Simplistically, I look at the world through a Red perspective and Andy looks at it with a Green view. Now by using the map, I can also say, what would this problem look like from a Green perspective, or with a Blue view or a Yellow filter. By using the map, my thinking can be free from the limits of my own perspective and I can expand my view to imagine what it may be like from the perspective of each area of the map.

Like a parable, the map works well; as it is easy to remember, makes you think and gives great insight.

In the next chapter, we will take a closer look at the different Interests that Dr Birkman identified and how they make up the first perspective of your unique Personality.

Simple is good, but we are complex

The map, like the stick drawing of the tree, is a simple way of remembering these basic principles. Guessing which colour you are, is a helpful start, but you are far too complex to be reduced to one colour. In the following chapters we will drill down into layers of complexity using a number of different perspectives

Focusing on the map: -

In this and subsequent chapters I have provided key learning points, one from each of the four colours of the map as well as the central position. You may well find that one or two of these learning points resonate with you more strongly than the others, this may add to your understanding of your own unique perspective.

Red corner: -	The map is a practical way of remembering this information, learn it and use it.
Green corner: -	The map and its colours can help you to articulate your uniqueness as well as other people's differences. This will help you communicate more effectively with other people and show you how you can get the best from them.
Blue corner: -	Creating a better future is much easier if you use the map and the colours. They provide a beautiful insight that will help you think about your uniqueness, other peoples' differences and how they complement you.
Yellow corner: -	The map provides a clear logical structure for understanding your unique Personality built on accurate historical data.
Central: -	The map helps you identify the nature of the different personalities, especially when you consider the behaviours that may occur at the extreme corners of the map.

4

God weaves Interests into your Personality

"So God created mankind in his own image, in the image of God he created them; male and female he created them."

Genesis.1 v27

People like to talk about having strengths. This is not unreasonable, but it does have an inherent problem, because when we talk of strengths then we find we must also talk about weaknesses. Because we see weakness as negative, we end up attributing positive and negative values to what are really just different aspects of Personality. As Christians this can be particularly problematic. If we aren't careful with the way we view Personality, we can fall into the trap of equating weakness with sin, which is very unhelpful.

If we see our personalities as God-given gifts, then I will have one 'gift' that you don't have and you will have a 'gift' that I do not have. Your absence of a gift is not a bad thing, it is a different thing.

God-given Personality is neither good nor bad

but each one is different

Each Personality is different. Different gifts may be more helpful in certain contexts, for example if your Personality really delights in the technical or mechanical aspects of life, you will be motivated to make things work. Others may find having to fix something really draining and have no desire to tinker in order to make something work – but this is OK. There is a clear difference, but of themselves, neither are 'good' or 'bad' - they are simply different. However, differences in Personality are more or less effective depending upon the context – if your computer needs fixing, then one of these two personalities is definitely happier and probably more effective than the other.

Dr Birkman, when developing his tool, was determined to get away from a language that was judgemental or labelled Personality elements as good or bad. The moral issue of what is 'good or bad' should be reserved for understanding our Character.

Understanding our differences, enables each one of us to play to our unique strengths in whichever way God has made our Personality. Undertaking a role that fits or matches your unique God-given Personality, will be much more successful than striving to carry out a role that you were simply not made for.

Energising Interests that shape our passions

The first perspective we need to get to grips with is our 'Interests'. All the areas of Interest that Dr Birkman identified, refer to things outside of our physical bodies in the world around us. There will be some Interests that energise you and ignite your passion; we give these a higher score, perhaps over 70 up to 99.

Other areas will exhaust or drain your energy and we score those low below 30 down to zero. Middle scores are simply ok things, neither energising nor draining.

It is worth noting that while you may recognise something of yourself in some of the descriptions that I will share with you, other people won't necessarily know that they are true about you, because Interests are often invisible to other people. When you come to understand your individual Interests, you can then explain them so that they can understand and respond to you much more effectively. In fact one of the most helpful things about this approach is that it provides you with a useable language that enables you to explain your Interests to other people.

Dr Birkman found it was possible to accurately describe and measure a person's Interests in a range of different areas that are physically outside of them. Examples will include; persuading others, being outdoors, creating art or organising or structuring an event. You will find that Interests will either be really stimulating and energising; unimportant, or very draining, dependent upon your Personality. Some will be areas where you can happily put your energy and passion and find them very rewarding. Some may be so important to you, that you discover they are essential to have in some part of your life. Others may be so draining, that even the thought of doing them makes you feel exhausted. High scoring Interests may not obviously seem to fit with your work or the roles that you undertake in Church, but they are so important that you should make sure you find time to understand and engage with them, because they are things that God has put in you.

Knowing your Interests does not guarantee that you will be particularly successful in that area, but when you discover your unique Interests and are free to invest time and effort into them, then any talent that you do have, will have every opportunity to grow.

A set of measurable Interests that God weaves into us

In the following paragraphs, we will explore each of the ten areas of Interest that Dr Birkman identified. Of course, there are areas of your Personality which are not included, such as a sense of humour, or a passion for collecting things and not to mention such complex things as sexuality. However, the measures we do have are more than enough to be really useful. As you read the following chapters some will resonate with you, others will not. Being aware of how you react to each example, will start to show you how you are unique.

To see or to be outdoors (Red)

You might be a person that feels most comfortable when outdoors and will take every opportunity to be in an open space. You will love to have a view of outdoors, or better still be in it. If there is no external view, such as a window revealing a skyscape, then a landscape painting or poster is better than a plain wall or abstract image. You may well see God in terms of His natural creation and find climbing a hill to pray gives you a much more intimate time with God than an enclosed room. He meets you in nature because He knows that's how He made you.

If you are asked to undertake a role that is in a small room that has no view, then you may find it very draining. One church moved its Sunday meeting into an old cinema, several people said after the trial period, that they found it oppressive, which made it hard to worship. The leadership felt they were just being difficult for no good reason and pressed on and moved in. If the Church had understood, that they were people with a high outdoor score, they might have been more considerate of a real need in those individuals.

Prayer walks through neighbourhoods or open air worship are likely better ways for you to meet with other Christians. If you have to undertake an indoor or confining role, you can manage it better if you supplement it with a good dose of being or seeing outdoors. Likewise if you have a very low score, then the idea of a prayer walk out on the hills, or a summer camp might be very unattractive.

Getting your hands on the technical or mechanical problem (Red)

Technical and mechanical people love to make things work, to make sure that no matter what a thing or event is, it does what it is supposed to do. If you have technical Interests you are likely to get stuck-in or hands on if something is broken - you take the spanner, the screwdriver or whatever tool is necessary to get the thing working again. In church you can be very distracted if things don't work as expected, or perhaps more likely you will just get on and fix what is wrong. This can run you into difficulties if the broken element is someone else's responsibility – especially if they don't have the same drive to fix it that you do.

You are likely to see God as the creator who makes everything work, and love the way God's hand is sovereignly working all things together for good for those that love Him. In fact, you may feel very close to God when admiring a beautiful steam engine or some other machine, because it reflects God's creativity and the beauty of how things work. God will meet you there because that's how He created you.

Some years ago, a pastor and good friend started teasing me, saying that I was wearing my red underpants on the outside, 'Superman style'. Whenever I tried to fix things that were not my responsibility, he would graciously remind me that I was wearing my Superman pants again and I should take them off. I have a much more balanced approach now, but still can leap towards fixing the problem if I am not careful. People with a low score might see such high score people as interfering and high scoring people may see those people who do not get things fixed as lazy. Once you realise that we are considering Personality difference, we then have an alternative to simply making judgemental comments about behaviour.

Please let me persuade you with my explanation (Green)

People with a persuasive Interest love talking with others and telling them a story. If this is you, you are probably very good at helping others to see what is in God's word, or explaining the gospel to those who don't understand it. You will talk with anyone that will listen and there is something very satisfying when people change their view having talked with you. This is especially true if it is something new and fresh - is it you who keeps pressing for new songs?

There are many roles in church that need this strength, from welcoming people, to sharing God's word. You probably see God as a communicator, speaking through His word or the words of others, speaking through songs; encouraging, comforting, bringing fresh revelation every day. There is nothing better than when God speaks with you, other than perhaps telling everyone else what God has been saying. God meets you in conversation because He made you to love speaking as He loves speaking.

If you have a low score here then you may well think that such persuasive people are trying to dominate conversation or even take advantage of you. It is easy to slip into a judgemental criticism of someone who is just being the Personality God made them to be.

I love to serve my society (Green)

You may find that you are drawn towards and are energised, by helping people with needs, whether directly or perhaps quite indirectly. This might be to help others to learn or grow, or to achieve a goal or perhaps assist with a physical need. This Social Service Interest, often appears with people who choose to be a Teacher or Social worker, a Counsellor or perhaps in Human Resources. You may enjoy listening to and encouraging others and find that prayer ministry is very satisfying for you. However, you express it, you will want to work with people and to be a blessing to them.

For You, God is the mighty King who is our help in troubles, our comforter and our counsellor. He is the God who has compassion for the poor, the leper, the lost and the dejected.

The story that Jesus gave in Luke 10 v25 of the Good Samaritan may be particularly meaningful to you. It's when you're helping others that you feel closest to God, because that's how He designed you.

If this is not you, then you might see such people as far too pre-occupied with people and not getting the job done, whatever that task might be.

As an example of how the Interests interact, consider what a person may look like if they have a high Social Services score AND a high Outdoor score, such a person may gravitate towards running a summer camp. If you have a high Social Service score AND a low Outdoor score, then you may well gravitate to running the Friday evening club in the hall. By understanding how you are made, you can start to fine tune where you put your effort and energy.

Isn't that a beautiful sight! (Blue)

Artistic people see beauty in the things around them; it is not enough that something should be functional and practical when it can be beautiful too. Colours, patterns and the impression an image makes, all speak to you and feed the creativity inside that wants to shape the world around you into something more beautiful. You have no problem with the idea of planting an avenue of trees knowing you will not see them fully-grown, because you can already see them grown in your mind's eye.

You will see God in the marvel and beauty of creation, you will see the beauty in words and songs that conjure up clear and powerful images. For you, the flower arrangement in the church meeting place, the design of a building, or the shape of a teapot, all speak to you of God's beauty. This is where God meets you, because His creativity is reflected in you.

Some people who have a low score here, simply don't get it and think that beauty is not practical or functional and therefore pointless.

Yet we know God loves beauty which lifts us and brings us closer to Him. Seeing beauty raises faith, as Jesus said,

> *"Consider the lilies of the field, how they grow: they neither toil nor spin, yet I tell you even Solomon in all his glory was not arrayed like one of these"*

> Mathew. 6 v28

You should not be surprised that many other people do not see what you see. Some people may stare blankly at you when you say that you want to create an artistic piece that will be an expression of the beauty of Jesus, but it may simply be they have a low Artistic score. If they are more technical or outdoor oriented they are less likely to understand or be passionate about the artistic and the abstract.

If you help them to understand that we are all uniquely created by God with different Interests, and therefore it is not surprising that they are bewildered by your Artistic passion, then you may find it a little easier to get permission from them to be creative.

I have finished writing, time for a good read (Blue)

Literary people are passionate about words and language, whether they are spoken, sung or written. Why use a word when you can better express meaning with a sentence; or perhaps find an unusual but accurate word? As well as words, you probably appreciate abstract ideas and concepts that you read about (and you probably read a lot).

God's written word is very important to you and other texts that explore and expand meaning help you to see God in the words. This is not surprising as Jesus is God's Word and it was the Word that brought about creation and brought all things into being (John. 1 v14). You may love singing, but it is the lyrics that stick far more than the melody.

God meets with you in words, it is where you feel close to Him and that is because God made you like that.

You may become quite frustrated when other people use words so casually and leave so much ambiguity. It may be that the person has a low Literary score, if so, then they do not see the imprecision of their language and may easily dismiss a badly formed phrase as being insignificant. Remembering that many other people do not value words in the same way as you do, can help you to be patient with what seems like a poor language skill. You can learn to gently lead them and show them a better way of articulating the meaning they are trying to impart. Of course you have to forgive and tolerate the 'ooos' and 'ah's' and 'yes yes yes' of some songs. The songwriter may have a high Musical score while also having a low Literary score. Also remember that a person with a low Interest here, may easily dismiss you as verbose and failing to 'simply say it as it is'.

Listening to the heartbeat of a song (Blue)

You may be passionate about music, and like the Artistic and Literary people described above, you love the creativity that comes with your passion. You love the melody and the rhythm, the tempo and even the 'colours' that music creates in your mind. The shape and rhythm of poetry and the song of the spoken word are all meaningful to you. The sound of water on a shingle beach may have a different set of meanings to you than water breaking on the sand, whereas a person with a low score may not notice the difference. To be able to stop and listen to the subtleties of nature is a delight to you. Indoors you will notice the sound of the air-conditioning or the noise of men working down the road, and they all add to the mix that you are very aware of and that others may not notice at all.

You meet God in a great tune or even in the delight of a quality tick of a clock. Every sound has meaning, because that is how God made you. Psalms with their great words form melody as you read them and the spoken word creates its own tune. The Bible is full of trumpets and drums and angels singing and when we worship we can't help but burst into song. Psalm 100 is close to you as it starts with *'make a joyful noise to the Lord'*.

When the music is wrong, too loud or the wrong tempo, you notice and it can be a real distraction. The dreadful feedback when a sound loops from the speaker into a microphone until it squeals can be genuinely painful to you. Getting others to understand this can be very difficult, as from their point of view they simply don't see or hear the issue.

As with Artistic and Literary Interests, many people will not understand your passion. For example, some people in church who are very practical can find themselves operating the public-address system. Their mechanical and practical approach might work technically, but when that comes without passion for creativity in music, it can really flatten what the music group is trying to produce for God's Glory. The best sound engineers have both Technical/Mechanical **and** Music Interests as they can understand what the musicians are trying to achieve and can use the technology to make it work. This combination is less common, so you have to look hard to find them. I at least make sure that the technical team are part of the worship team, to help them understand the team's creativity.

The logical delight of numbers (Yellow)

You might be a person that is passionate about numbers and using mathematics and logic to analyse and solve problems and puzzles. For you Sudoku is more attractive than crosswords. You enjoy measuring and other logical tasks such as breaking codes or even knitting, each of which have a numerical base behind them. Bookkeeping and accounts are not a chore for you rather there is delight in balancing the books to the last penny. Projects and plans, which at first may not seem numerical, can benefit from your logical approach, but you may struggle with those creative people who seem to have no logic to their thinking at all.

You meet God in the logic and order of the world and in some of the astounding numbers that are clearly important to God. The Trinity is a perfect number and relationship. Jesus had twelve apostles but refers to three that he loves.

Seven appears frequently as a perfect number stemming from God's creation and His rest on the seventh day. For you these numbers can be very meaningful.

While you find God in the logic, those people who are more driven by feelings may see your numerical rationale as being a little heartless. Of course, this is not true, but it may often be how you are perceived by others who are different from you.

The structure and order of a tidy mind (Yellow)

People with a clerical or administrative Interest are ordered, structured and thrive on managing information and organising how knowledge is stored and accessed. You may well have a clear system for the order of your books or CD's on your shelf, perhaps by number or by author or by genre. You find filing systems very satisfying and may delight in undertaking a stock check, knowing that you have planned just the right amount of tea and coffee for the month and finding your plan was spot on.

You may meet God in the order of the universe and in ordered worship, that is how He has made you and it reflects that He is a God of order. God did not simply create the world, He had a clear sequence, from His first words commanding 'Light!' to His final act of creating humans in His image, before resting. Psalm 100 shows a pattern to worship:

> *Enter his gates with thanksgiving and his courts with praise; give thanks to him and praise his name.*

> Psalm. 100 v4

Modern churches may encourage freedom of expression in worship, which is a delight for many people, but you see beauty in the structure, which is why liturgy and ceremony can be very attractive to you, not because they are a legalistic ritual, but because they reflect the God-given order to things.

People who do not have this Interest are likely to be very people focused compared to you, so they may easily misunderstand your passion for order, as not caring for people, this of course is not true, you simply put the structure before the people. But you have to keep a close watch that you do not fall into a pattern for the pattern's sake.

If you have Interests in both Numerical and Administrative areas, then you are likely to want to focus on the task at hand and keep discussion to a minimum. Of course, you need other people, and yet, just as Jesus took time out to be alone to pray, you also know the comfort of being alone with God.

I am curious and I need to understand why (Red/Blue)

You may delight in the scientific understanding of how things work and in the physical laws that God has ordained in nature. For you there is a marvel in the way the complex interaction of chemicals work together in the body, or the way metals can be blended to make stronger materials, or the way that light, x-rays or gravity have such fixed natural laws. You may rejoice in how subtle changes to a recipe can create a delightful dish, or how trees turn light into energy. Whatever the subject, you need to know and cannot resist asking why? How does this work? What happens if we try this or that?

You find God in the natural laws of the universe as He is in all things and holds them in His hand, reflecting something of God's knowledge and understanding as He holds and maintains the universe in ways we cannot comprehend.

In your life and at church you want to examine and explore because you need to understand. When others are developing plans, you are able to keep asking the 'why' question, in order to expand understanding and drive out assumptions and help others to understand their rationale and their aim. You can bring focus to the **'why** they are doing, **what** they are doing'.

If someone has a low Scientific score then they will probably find it difficult to grasp why you are so passionate about understanding the world, and by that very nature they do not need to understand those people who 'really do need to know why'. When you explain to people with a low scientific score that some people are not like them, then you can both start to grasp the benefits of your differences.

The Scientific Interest is fascinating, in that it can interact with any of the other Interests - especially with Outdoor, Mechanical, Artistic, Literary and Musical. So for example if you have Interest in Music and Science then you will want to understand harmonics and wave lengths and their theories or how a wind instrument creates the sound that makes it beautiful or ugly – this may not be of Interest to someone who isn't scientific by nature.

Life experiences can blind us to the Interests that God has placed in us

Recognising that people are each created quite differently, with such a broad mix of Interests, can be a hard concept to grasp. The following is an example of how understanding your Interests can be very important, and, as in this example, it can be life changing.

I worked with a Charity that was attached to a church who taught English to refugees. One teacher had been off work sick, for some 6 out of the previous 12 months, when she approached her manager saying she wanted to quit. She was a good teacher and her manager could not understand what was happening so she asked me to step-in and try and make sense of what was going on.

The 'Social Service' Interest we mentioned above, relates to working with people who are in a position that leaves them with needs. If you have a high score for 'Social Service' then you would be energised by working with such a clearly needy group. However, this teacher had a very low score, implying she would find such work draining. If she was teaching a group that were not so needy and enjoyed learning, she may have found it a little easier. Her sick record was starting to make sense.

The teacher's highest Interest score was in 'Numerical', i.e. working with numbers and patterns, so, along with many other things, I took opportunity to turn the conversation towards working with numbers and doing maths activities, anything that was numerical in origin. Despite her scores, the teacher was adamant, saying "No, I don't do maths!"

At first, I could not understand why she was denying this subject so emphatically, when it was clearly an area she would be energised by. After some time talking, I found out that her father was a Professor of Maths and her sister was a Doctor of Maths. Compared with most people, she was really good, but when she compared herself with those closest to her, she thought she was rubbish. Once we had gently worked through this discussion, the light came on and she now works as a bookkeeper, is undertaking accountancy training and is very happy indeed.

So in this case, not only had she denied the one key area where she was designed to be passionate, but she'd invested in a specific people group, refugees, that completely drained her energy.

Understanding this she was able to positively change her focus to match her Interests and was much, much happier as a result.

You might say, 'surely working with refugees and asylum seekers is very important work?' and you would be right, especially for a Christian wanting to emulate Christ's compassion. However, if God designed you in a way that you find such work exhausting and someone else finds it energising, then who do you think will do the best job?

When we are influenced by others to do a good work that we are not designed for, we can end up doing an important job quite badly. No wonder that this lady felt so miserable that it made her ill.

Whilst her ingrained beliefs (part of her 'Character') said 'this is important compassionate work, you must do it,' her Personality was saying 'this is simply exhausting I am not designed for this'.

Perhaps, one day, that ex-teacher will be able to use the accountancy skills she is developing, in a similar charity, bringing alignment to her Character and Personality.

This happens to be a work example, but in truth there is little difference between a secular role that God leads you to and a church role. Either may be paid or unpaid, it makes no difference. What does make a difference, is what God is asking you to contribute your time and effort too and how that fits with the Personality He has given you. The most effective and productive things you can do are where the task matches your Interests, because then the task itself will energise you and give you greater motivation to press on.

Combining two areas of Interest

As your understanding of these different Interests grows, you will start to see how they interact. For example, one Pastor I know who has a high Persuasive score of 90 loves talking to other people - he never stops talking unless he is asleep! He also has a Technical score of 12. His house is falling apart. He has always had a policy of moving house after five years because that's when things start dropping of the walls and get seriously bad. He currently has a loose sink and tiles coming off the bathroom wall. Of course, there is no excuse for not getting the house fixed, but with such a low mechanical score, he should definitely not be the person to fix it. He will make it worse. He needs to persuade (or pay) others to do the work while he continues to put effort into his role as a Pastor - where he shines.

It is ok to be gifted more in one area than in another and as he gradually accepts this, he will become increasingly more comfortable with letting those who have a high technical/mechanical score fix his house.

Now imagine the score were reversed high Mechanical and low Persuasive. How do you think these Interests might affect such a person? He will probably be putting effort into tinkering with his car or making a boat in his basement. He is also probably a person of few words. If both scores were high then he would probably be the man in the repair shop who fixes your computer and tells you his life history at the same time.

You can see here, that even by knowing just two areas of Interest we can start to see how they may interact and what the impact of such Interests might have on your Personality.

How Social Service Interest can trip up Christians

This Interest in helping needy people, is one that can cause Christians to stumble, unless we really understand it well. The Bible is full of commands to 'do for one another', whether that is to pray, help, feed or protect. We are taught in society and especially in church, that we should help others. Of course, at one level this is true, we should. However, there is a difference between helping when we see a need and making a vocation out of helping. A key question here is, do you have a passion to help needy people because God made you like that by placing this Interest into your Personality, or have you learned to help needy people because it is socially a good thing to do?

The story of the Good Samaritan is actually helpful here when we stop and consider the detail. We do not know what the Samaritan did for a living, but it is not likely that he was a health-care professional. He saw a need, had compassion on the poor man and did what he could. He arranged with a hospitable Inn-keeper for the injured man to be looked after, fed and have his wounds tended to. He made provision for this by giving some money and agreeing to pay any more needed when he would return in a few days. The Inn-keeper trusted the Samaritan enough to agree with this arrangement. Perhaps he had done this before? The Samaritan went back to his job. He did not make the poor man his pet project, he did not take up caring for a living, he simply trusted the task to someone he believed would do the job better than he could. This suggests that the Samaritan knew when he had done enough.

This ability to know we have done enough and to be content, is something we can really struggle with.

The Samaritan met the need

but did not turn this into a vocation

Many Christians I have met and worked with, feel guilty that they should be doing more to help other people. However, if you have a low Social Service score, then God did not design this into you. Therefore, be like the Good Samaritan and be compassionate, help in the moment and then pass them on to someone who will do a better job than you can. Perhaps that person will actually thrive when they are helping others.

There is no reason to feel guilty if you have not been designed to help needy people, because you will have different passions that can be used to bless others in different ways.

When you discover your unique Interests, be that with numbers or structure, music, art or literature, understanding and fixing things or persuading people to help, whatever your gifts, then of course you can turn that ability towards blessing and helping other people. But if you build a vocation on something that drains you dry, then it will be a disaster for you, God did not make you to be like that.

Is my Personality an excuse for avoiding difficult things?

Imagine you have high Yellow Interests such as in Numbers and Administration. You could say that this is your key passion and where you find satisfaction. As a result, you have no real desire to engage with people. However, we are social beings and especially in church were God may speak to us through other people. You cannot use your introverted passion to avoid taking with others.

Likewise, if you have high Green Interests such as Persuasion, you cannot use your passion to talk with people to avoid completing key paperwork. You might find it hard, but such things are unavoidable, so you cannot use your personality as an excuse for avoiding your responsibilities

This is why you need to get your head round the difference. Being honest about your Personality does not give your Character the right to use your Personality as a weapon. We must learn to **be** the people we are meant to be, with Christ's Character.

That is why we are human **be**ings and not human **do**ings

The Unique you

The above descriptions give you insight into the areas where you have God-given passions. Where you strongly resonate with two or three areas of Interests, then those are likely to be the areas you should be putting your energy and effort, because they will energise you. There will also be areas to avoid if you can, as they will drain you dry. If you have to put effort into areas that you would prefer to avoid, then try to add-in activity with an energising Interest to give you a boost.

> We assume people are rather like us until we learn
> otherwise

Be aware that you are the only one with your exact mix of Interests. This means that other people may not immediately understand you. We all tend to view others through our own perceptions; therefore we assume people are rather like us until we learn otherwise. Sometimes these assumptions can be very wrong leading to conflicts with others or even within our own mind. If someone paints a picture of how you should behave, or worse still, states that 'this is how a good Christian is', then the assumptions they put into that picture may fit them well and yet fit you very badly indeed.

Don't try to adopt your heroes' Personality, rather find the unique Personality God has created in you.

Take a guess at the areas that motivate your passion

Having read through the ten different areas of Interest, take a few minutes to score each one out of ten – ten where the Interest is very strong for you down to zero where you have no Interest at all.

	Score	Highest 3	Lowest 3
• Outdoor.			
• Technical/Mechanical.			
• Persuasive.			
• Social Service.			
• Artistic.			
• Literary.			
• Musical.			
• Numerical.			
• Administrative.			
• Scientific.			

Now tick your three highest scores and the three lowest scores.

Consider how they interact with each other to shape your unique Personality. How do you invest energy into these Interests in your life, work and in your church?

Are you putting your time and effort into things that you are naturally made to be more passionate about?

Then tick the bottom three (which will be the most draining areas) and consider how they interact to shape your Personality.

Think about your life, your roles at work or in church. Are you required to undertake work in these areas? If so, try adding in some tasks from those areas that will energise you. You may even need to consider if you're undertaking the right roles in the first place? Perhaps it is time for a change? But don't leap just yet, remember you are guessing here, if you're considering a significant change, perhaps you should get properly measured with an assessment first?

Focus on Interests: -

Red corner: -	Identify your Interests and invest your energy into the top areas. Avoid Interests that drain you.
Green corner: -	Understand your high and low score Interests and tell others about them. It will be much easier for you to succeed with the people around you if they understand you better. Persuade others to address the areas which God did not design into you.
Blue corner: -	Give yourself time to understand your creative and strategic thinking. Delight, as God does, in your ability to express things to others, in ways that many people cannot.
Yellow corner: -	Recognise that you can see and bring order in ways that others cannot. Plan how to use your list of Interests and the things that drain you. God delights in your plan especially when it matches His.
Central: -	Delight in your ability to see how Interests work in different people, embrace all your high score Interests and recognise that God makes some people much more extreme than you.

5

Things that your Personality Needs

Do not let any unwholesome talk come out of your mouths, but only what is helpful for building others up according to their needs, that it may benefit those who listen.

Ephesians. 4 v29

In the last two chapters, we looked at Interests which are areas, outside of us, that motivate or drain us of energy. Needs are different, in that they are the things we need from our environment and the people we interact with, in order that we can be our useful selves.

In chapter 3 we asked you to guess which of the four colours resonated the most with you and then asked you to mark it on the map that you have drawn. As an overall summary this is useful. However, like the stick and squiggle drawing of a tree, it is only a starting place. As we then learn the difference between deciduous and evergreen trees; which trees produce fruit and nuts we can eat and those we can't, our understanding of trees gradually becomes more detailed and nuanced.

In the same way, when we look at people, we must learn that by taking different perspectives, we can start to understand the complexity of each individual.

For example, in chapter 4, I showed you that when all of my Interests are summed together, then the Red area best describes my Interests. Now we dig down a little further into a second perspective that God placed within us, things that we Need. When our individual Needs are summed together, they produce a new and different perspective on the map - you will see from the map below, that my Needs are Blue.

Most personality assessments that you might use, only give one perspective and consequently, if you do the assessment twice, you can receive very different results, depending on which aspects of your Personality come to the fore each time. The Birkman Method® assessment is the only tool that gives you a set of different perspectives on one map, describing these different aspects of your Personality.

In the map below, you can see that I have Red Interests (the asterisk) and Blue Needs, shown by the circle.

Most people will find that their Interests and Needs are either horizontally or vertically related to their Needs on the map. Less frequently you will find them diagonally related, as mine are.

Some people will have their Interests and Needs close to each other, or even in the same colour of the map.

Consequently, you now have to consider your Personality as being more complex than the one perspective. Now you have to ask yourself, what colour are my Interests and what colour are my Needs? What impact do the differences between them show me about my Personality?

Like the Interests, Needs are grouped into the same four colours. Below you will find a broad description of the common things people Need, within each of the four colours of the map.

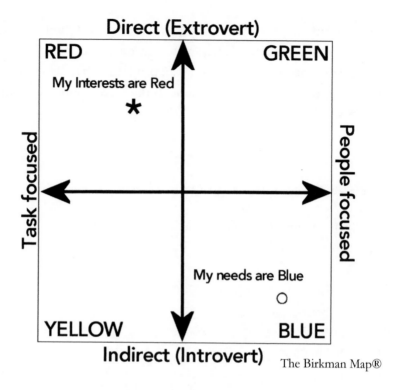

The Birkman Map®

Just a minute - I thought you are a Red person?

It's all about perspective! My Interests are described as Red, however, when you look at my Needs, you will find that they are Blue. I am a Red person from one perspective and a Blue person from a different perspective. In chapter 7 we will explore a third perspective where I am different again. Therefore, I am 'Blue' from one perspective and 'Red' from another.

Grasping this idea of perspectives is the first big step in understanding the complexity of our personalities. Within each perspective lie a vast range of details and elements of each of the four colours - every person is unique.

Take a computer printer for example, which has just four ink colours; red, blue, yellow and black. As your computer selects a mix with different amounts of each colour, it can produce 100 million different colours. In the same way the four Birkman colours, with three perspectives can describe billions of different personalities.

Understanding something of your Needs

Read through the descriptions and then think about which colour group is the closest description to what you feel you Need.

You should be able to recognise and associate your Needs with one colour of the map, although some people will feel they have a balance of two areas. This occurs if your Needs are on the border of two colours of the map.

Occasionally you find people who feel they equally associate with three or four sets of needs, which can occur if your Needs are close to the centre of the cross of the map.

You will find that referring to the different colours and the general attributes described below helps to reinforce the usefulness of the map.

People with Red Needs

God made people with Red Needs to be like Himself, that is, they Need to be active and decisive and to be busy with plenty to do. Rather than vague or ambiguous instructions, Red people Need clear cut decisions from other people. Consequently, they are happier when others provide clarity about information or tasks, finding it difficult if people are uncertain with them.

Don't talk about the idea or concept of a brick, just give them a brick, a tangible response that they can see and understand. When giving information or tasks to them, give it to them straight with the minimal amount of padding - they Need you to get to the point.

Church life is positive for people with Red Needs if they have plenty of clear tasks to do. They do best when the worship is clear and to the point and the preaching of the Word clearly leads to actions that work. Vague prayers are frustrating, prayers that say what they mean and have a clear focus, are much more engaging. Don't ask them to do things that require careful diplomacy or subtlety, or you will make them seem like 'a bull in a china shop'. God did not make them for subtlety or for being especially pastoral. Don't ask people with Red Needs to tread softly in a situation, but tell them what to do.

People with Green Needs

God made people with Green Needs to be like Himself, that is, to engage and talk with people. God is the 'Great I am' and those with Green Needs also know they are unique individuals. Green Needs people Need opportunities to discuss and to debate, and Need relationships where they can be competitive with others. They also Need variety, novelty and frequent changes of activity as well as freedom to be independent. They Need to be free from traditions or precise rules.

When giving information or tasks to them, be clear that they can see the benefits to themselves as they really do Need to win.

Church life is positive for people with Green Needs if they are free to talk with people. Opportunities to undertake evangelism or sharing the word, where they can influence others into gaining salvation or a further step in their walk with Christ, can be really satisfying for them. Worship that speaks to God or to the people is a delight. When the Word is shared demonstrating the clear advantages of engaging with the grace of God, they can be really fulfilled. Praying with freedom is a delight to them whereas a formal list can be as dry as anything. God made Green Needs people with the requirement to bless and help other people and there are plenty of opportunities to do this - but don't ask them to undertake repetitive tasks or even to fix things because God may not have made them for that.

People with Blue Needs

God made people with Blue Needs to be like Himself, that is, to be thoughtful and creative. Blue Needs people Need time to consider and reflect before making decisions, and to take time to be in a still quiet place. They Need to develop clear strategies to secure the future for themselves and others. They thrive on having genuine friendships that last a lifetime and are not demanding, and find social demands quite difficult and wearing.

When giving information or tasks to them, suggest an outline and allow some space for ambiguity, allowing them to be creative.

Church life is positive for people with Blue Needs if there is freedom to express themselves creatively without putting them in the spotlight. Worship that has space for creativity is a delight, whereas formal rigid worship can be stifling. If the Word is presented in fresh and creative ways, it is easy to engage with, and likewise prayer flows more easily when there is space to create and express themselves. Never put Blue Needs people on the spot by asking them for an instant response in the middle of a meeting, they will simply clam-up.

People with Yellow Needs

God made people with Yellow Needs to be like Himself, that is to be factual and precise with a clear structure and plan. Yellow Needs people require a clear logical schedule and plan to work with, to know exactly what needs to be done. They are happiest when they clearly know who is in charge and when the rules are precisely explained and unequivocal. It is important they feel part of the group but not in an overtly emotional way.

When giving information or tasks to Yellow Needs people, be clear and logical. Give time frames that are accurate whenever possible and avoid vague statements. Even if 'next month' is clear enough for you, something which is more accurate, such as 'at the end of the second week', will suit a person with Yellow Needs better.

Church life is positive for people with Yellow Needs, if they have a clear understanding of the order of things and those things have a logical progression. Worship flows well for them, if they know the songs well, whereas vague contemplative songs can be frustrating. Traditional worship can be very comforting because if the song has a long history, then this shows it has stood the test of time. The Word is best received when it follows a clear plan; if a speaker keeps going down tangents they can easily lose sight of the plan and find it frustrating. The prayer life of someone with Yellow Needs may have a consistent pattern to it. Yellow people are quite likely to be able to quote their favourite prepared prayer such as those Jesus taught His disciples or written down by historical figures. Even if they are asked to pray out in a meeting, they will be more comfortable having advance notice, so they can write it down and ensure it is logical and correctly formed.

Meeting all the Needs all the time

Most churches will want to be attractive to the complete range of people. It is hard to meet the above four different sets of Needs in any simple formula. In fact, whilst a formula might bless the Yellow people, the majority of others may hate it! Some churches choose to only address one or two types of people, whether by freely soaking in the Holy Spirit or following a traditional format, or indeed any one of the many available models.

The problem with these approaches is that it is easy to adopt a style which only attracts one or two of the colour groups. Consequently, you can find you're building a lop-sided church.

If you're not aware of your bias

you will build a lop-sided church

A biased church walks with a limp, but even worse is the church which attempts to please all through compromises that lead to an insipid 'lowest common-denominator', as the Bible warns: -

> *'I know your deeds, that you are neither cold nor hot. I wish you were either one or the other! So, because you are lukewarm—neither hot nor cold—I am about to spit you out of my mouth.'*

Revelations. 3 v15-16

We need to build churches that are 'Hot' for God, where everyone is motivated and engaged. To do this means making sure that the church meets all four colour Needs if it is to engage with all of the people. Understanding the principles in this book is the start of a journey of building a church which engages all sorts of different people.

As we continue through the different chapters you will keep seeing that some things apply to you and others do not. Equally important then, is that this means some people may have some similarities to you whilst others show significant Personality differences. As your understanding of this grows you can then learn to adapt how you behave, enabling you to account for these differences.

This is a significant benefit with any group of people in church or work life. Valuing and engaging with differences brings a much healthier and productive environment for everyone.

What happens if your Needs do not get met?

It is important here to stop and acknowledge that what we have been describing are Needs, not just preferences or likes. They are not things that your physical body needs, or indeed desires that may appear in your Character. They are things that your Personality Needs in order to function well. If you do not have these Needs met over a period of time, over some weeks or even months, then you may find yourself starting to act in counterproductive ways. Other people may describe you as having lost the plot and can react with some incredulity, as they genuinely do not know what is going on with you. What is actually happening, is that you have started to try and get your key Needs met, but in a really unhelpful way. We call this 'Stress-Behaviour'. It is shown on the map by the square, which always appears in the same place as the Needs circle.

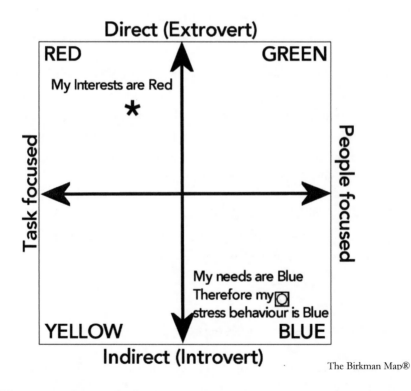

The Birkman Map®

Examples of stress behaviour

If you had met me a few years ago and got to know me, you would have found someone that is sociable and friendly, quite vocal at times, and always ready to give an answer or add to the conversation. However, I also Need time alone to digest and think things through.

I once attended a church conference with friends and, as they expected, I was busy and engaged with all that was going on. However, after a couple of days of full-on interactions, I met my limit and suddenly disappeared to get some space. Unfortunately, it was just when the other people at the conference needed me and were left wondering what on earth was going on!

The lack of time to think and reflect, combined with the Need for time alone, caused me to blow a fuse and take the afternoon off at entirely the wrong time. This was me in my stress behaviour, overwhelmed by the Need to be alone!

I've learnt from that experience and today I make sure that I plan time to be alone and reflect, so that I don't fall into that unhelpful stress-behaviour.

Stress behaviour is not simply feeling a bit stressed. When a core Need is not met then a person can demonstrate really unhelpful behaviour in a counterproductive attempt to get that Need met.

Whereas Needs can be quite hidden from other people, counterproductive Stress-Behaviour is seen by everyone in the vicinity. Seeing such behaviour is easy, but understanding it is much harder, especially when the behaviour turns out to be very different from what you usually see of that person.

Using the map to help you learn about Needs

The diagram below lays out the briefest summaries of each colour's Needs. The short statements are simply to remind you of the larger descriptions above. This map is similar to the discussion in chapter 4, but the perspective has changed.

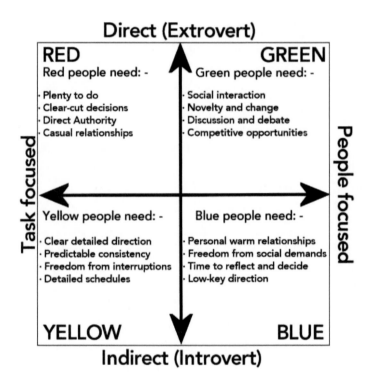

The Birkman Map®

Consider where you think your Needs might be and choose that colour and mark it on your map with a circle. Is it the same or different from your guess in chapter 4?

Now look at the description in the diagonal colour of the map. Try to think about someone you know whose Needs might fit that part of the map. This is not easy to do because Needs are often hidden, but you might be able to guess. If you can guess, then they are going to be quite different from you. Perhaps write their name on your map.

Now think about the other two colours and their descriptions. Again, not easy, but try to think of people you know who might match those colours. If you cannot think of anyone, then try thinking of your favourite TV characters and which area of the map you might put them in. The 'Star Trek Mr Spock' is a good example here, who shows he is Usually extremely logical but underneath has a real Need for others to address his emotions that are exceptionally supressed.

If you can, think about how you approach each of the three people you have added to the map. When you talk with them, do you treat them all the same or do you adjust how you behave with each one? If you treat everyone the same, you are probably treating them in the same way that you Need to be treated. This is natural behaviour, but you now know that they each have different Needs, so you can start treating each one as the unique person they are, doing the best you can to meet their Needs, because you know that that is what helps them shine and do well.

The detail behind the Needs map

Dr Birkman identified nine separate components within these Needs. Together these create your unique position on the map.

Each component can be drawn as a line, with each end having opposite meanings. A score of zero is just as intense as a score of ninety-nine, but with opposite meanings. The centre is a balance of both. While you can be near the centre and therefore be a balance of both meanings, you cannot be strongly at both ends.

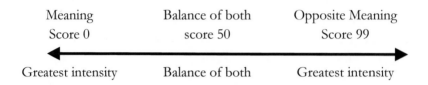

Meaning	Balance of both	Opposite Meaning
Score 0	score 50	Score 99

| Greatest intensity | Balance of both | Greatest intensity |

The nine measures that make up your Needs on the map, are described in the table below, describing the opposite ends of each measure.

You might ask which colour is associated with each statement, but this would simply complicate things at this stage. What is important is recognising the statements that reflect part of your Personality. Those that strongly resonate with you will resurface with you when you read the next chapter which reviews each Need in a little more detail.

Just as important as ascertaining your own Needs is recognising that others will have a different set of Needs from you. Being able to adapt your behaviour to help meet others Needs is really important. It is the difference between people complementing each other or being in conflict with each other.

Take a few minutes to read each description and then tick the box next to the statement that resonates the most with you. If both descriptions seem equally important to you then write a 'b' in the middle for balance of both.

Your guess about you, tick one of the ends that resonate most with you or put a **b** in the middle if both resonate equally.

Tick	Low Score	Name of Need	High Score	Tick
	Needs Individual goals and opportunities to work alone.	Social Energy.	Needs to be accepted as part of the group.	
	Needs to conserve energy reflecting and considering things at their own pace.	Physical Energy.	Needs to be active with practical results and physical action.	
	Needs logical facts, solutions, communications and practical tasks.	Emotional Energy.	Needs outlet for feelings, thoughts and close relationships in which to confide.	
	Needs frank and direct relationships.	Self-consciousness.	Needs sensitivity from others in One to One relationships.	
	Needs freedom from supervision, suggest rather than tell and minimum conflict.	Assertiveness.	Needs to know who is in charge and can be in charge if no one else is.	
	Needs freedom from close control, Needs variety and informal relationships.	Insistence.	Needs detailed structure, process and procedures.	

Derived from the Birkman Method®

Tick	Low Score	Name of Need	High Score	Tick
	Needs to serve and support team with minimum competitiveness.	Incentives.	Needs to compete and to win, with clear rules to competition.	
	Needs to be able to take immediate action prefers minimal ambiguity.	Thought.	Needs time to think; digest ideas and to consider and reflect before taking action.	
	Needs to be able to focus on task and protection from interruptions or sudden changes.	Restlessness.	Needs a variety of tasks, frequent changes and flexible routines.	
	The following do not translate on to the map.			
	Needs order and a predictable environment with well-established rules and procedures.	Freedom.	Needs freedom from social constraints and outside control. Needs opportunities to be non-conforming.	
	Needs achievable success and public approval.	Challenge.	Needs stretching challenges and opportunities to prove self.	

Derived from the Birkman Method®

Focus on your Needs: -

Red corner: -	Identify and ensure your Needs are met in order to perform well.
Green corner: -	By Identifying your Needs, you will be in a position to discuss your Needs with others, so that they can get the best from you and you from them.
Blue corner: -	When you identify your Needs and help others to meet them, you will be in a better place to consider and create a strategy for a better future.
Yellow corner: -	Recognising your unique set of Needs enables you to structure a clear plan to ensure your Needs are well met in order that you can perform as well as possible.
Central: -	A balanced set of Needs means you are likely to be able to invest energy into most areas, a 'Jack of all trades'.

6

How Needs impact People

'Let the wise listen and add to their learning, and let the discerning get guidance for understanding proverbs and parables, the sayings and riddles of the wise. The fear of the Lord is the beginning of knowledge, but fools despise wisdom and instruction.'

Proverbs. 1 v5-7

Using stories to illustrate knowledge and help people gain insight and wisdom is a well-established method. In order to place the descriptions of our Personality Needs into a meaningful context, the following stories explore each pair of Needs that Dr Birkman identified (you may need to refer back to the map and list in the previous chapter, to remind you of the short version descriptions).

As you read each story you will see two central people that have personalities at opposite ends of each measurable element. You may well find it easier to relate to one or the other, or in some cases, feel that you are a balance of both. It all depends on the unique Personality God has given you. Each tale is designed to help you see where Needs have an impact on behaviour.

The initial letter of each of the character's name corresponds with the initial letter of the colour of the map where that person's Need sits. William is 'white' and white describes a Personality that is close to the centre of the map.

A social animal?

Gina and Yvonne belong to the same bible study group and decide to start an eight-week course. Gina, a teacher, loves how such courses give real opportunity for discussion within the group. Yvonne, a bookkeeper, is much quieter than Gina and is also really looking forward to working through the well-structured study guide.

After a couple of weeks, Gina feels that while most people seem quite chatty and comfortable in sharing their opinions, Yvonne rarely adds to the conversation and sometimes moves to sit at a table on her own as she writes away at the questions. Gina asks Yvonne if she is alright and if she is enjoying the course. Yvonne responds very positively that she is enjoying it, but Gina doesn't understand why Yvonne doesn't contribute to the group, or why her little prompts to include Yvonne in the conversation are not making any difference.

Towards the end of one of these meetings Gina blurts out, "I think it is really important that we all contribute to the team. Do we all agree?" The room falls silent, surprised by Gina's outburst. They all know Gina to be a chatty and polite member of the group, so what's gone wrong?

Summary

Yvonne is Yellow, structured and ordered and very comfortable with her own company, so while she is happy to be part of the group, she doesn't Need it - in fact at times she Needs to be alone. Gina, on the other hand, *does* Need to know that she is part of the group and assumes everyone would feel the same about belonging and partaking in the discussion.

In this case Yvonne was not demonstrating that she was valuing the group in the same way Gina does. Gina lost certainty about them being a group at all, which over time created frustrations. That led to her counterproductive outburst, an attempt to bring her certainty that they were a group.

If Gina had understood Yvonne's Yellow Need to be alone in her work, she would have been much more relaxed. Working alone is not a criticism of the group; it is just what Yellow people Need.

If Yvonne had understood Gina's Green Need to belong and for the group to function together, she would have made the occasional reassuring comment about how she valued the group despite Needing some time alone.

Neither of the Needs are wrong, they are just different.

Too busy to be patient

William, a church Administrator, has just handed in his notice. The Pastors, Bruce and Raymond, are both disappointed: he has done all the administrative work efficiently, made a good impression with his communication skills, makes helpful contributions to the team's prayer times and can be quite practical. They decide to meet William and persuade him to stay.

Raymond starts off, "We don't want you to go, what can we do to make you stay?"

Bruce adds, "Yes, William, we really value your contribution to the church. Can you help us understand why you want to leave?"

William thinks for a moment. "It's nothing personal. I have enjoyed working here and learnt a lot. I just believe it is the right time to move on and get some wider experience."

"Well we could send you on some training courses that will be good for you." Raymond responds. "You could help me with the website and the autumn study programme. The summer camp has mountains of things that will need doing; we could release you from the office to help with that?"

"Thank you Raymond," William replies, "but it's not that I don't have enough to do already, it is a busy job."

Bruce spoke quickly so that he could get in before Raymond. "It sounds like maybe you're actually too busy and not getting time to recharge your batteries? Perhaps you could come along to the monthly prayer retreat? You would have plenty of time to pray and reflect or just sit and take in God's wonderful nature. How does that sound?"

William thought and replied, "Thank you Bruce, it's a very kind offer, but I think after a while I might get a bit fidgety. I can see you both want me to stay and I am flattered, thank you. But I am not like either of you. I feel God is guiding me to a different experience."

Summary

Raymond Needs to be busy and consequently he sees the world from this perspective - being busy is good because God loves to be busy;

He is a God of action. Bruce, on the other hand, Needs to conserve energy and only does things he knows need to be done. Conserving energy for when it's needed is good - God knows when to rest, which is why He rested on the seventh day. Bruce and Raymond's differences make it hard for them to understand one another at times.

William's Personality lies between those of the two Pastors, and while he will never be as busy as Raymond or as reflective as Bruce, he understands them both to a good degree.

A logical or emotional coffee?

Raymond and Bruce's church has been given a large sum of money to create a new café and kitchen within the church building, so they meet with an Architect, Winston, to develop the design.

Raymond tells Winston that, "We are looking for a very practical solution. It needs to be functional and easy to keep clean. It will be used by lots of different people, so it will need to be durable".

Bruce then added "Raymond is right of course, but what we really want is to draw people in and make them feel that this is a place they can stay and talk and soak up the atmosphere of modern church life. We want people to feel comfortable as they drink their coffee."

Winston thought for a moment. "I think I understand what you both need. The kitchen side needs to be both durable and easy to keep clean for the volunteers. At the same time, visitors need an environment with some of the space for practical eating areas and some of the space more like a coffee lounge where people can relax?"

Bruce said "Yes that's right, but the area needs to be calming and encouraging so that people can talk and the light needs to make the place look beautiful. Maybe we could involve some local artists in the decoration."

Raymond added "By all means talk with artists, but we need to make sure we don't get bogged down with endless thinking and ideas. We need to deliver something that will make a difference to people right now, not years into the future."

Winston thought for a moment. "Let me draft out some suggestions for you to look at. Maybe divide the workload, so that Raymond, your main focus could be on the kitchen and Bruce, your main focus on the public space. When we meet again I can show you something tangible that will help you get a feel for what I am thinking."

Summary

Raymond Needs to focus on the facts and believes the facts will speak for themselves. He will always consider the facts before he thinks about how the people might feel. Bruce, on the other hand, will think about people's feelings before getting round to the facts - indeed each fact is thought of in terms of the impact on people. This difference in perspective is both valid and useful, but if both are not considered, then a distorted view can easily be formed that can ignore either of the two valid views.

Getting to the point

Having started at the same time, neither Bruce nor Raymond would say they are senior to the other. After some months, they agreed that it was time to explore the Church Vision.

Raymond started. "Our vision needs to be practical and to the point."

Bruce replied, "Yes it needs to have clear application, but also needs to engage everyone. We need to pray and wait on God so that we're of one heart. We need to give the vision time to develop, so that we're really clear where we feel God's taking us."

"You're not suggesting that we're not of one heart are you?"

"No, we are of one heart," Bruce responded, "but I've noticed that you can sometimes get to the point rather quickly and I'm not sure you've got everyone with you when you've arrived."

"What do you mean?" asked Raymond, bluntly.

Bruce paused. "Well, I think that sometimes people lag behind you with their thinking. You're able to move very quickly through the facts and some of us find it hard to digest one statement before the next one has arrived."

"What are you saying?" said Raymond sounding frustrated.

Bruce replied, "I think what I'm trying to say is that sometimes you can be rather to the point, a bit direct, even a bit blunt. When sharing the vision, we need everyone to understand, so we need to take our time with it."

"Yes" said Raymond, "That's why the message must be clear."

"True, but let me put it another way. You are very good at taking the various ideas and boiling them all down to a very clear and direct message. Many people in the Church really value your ability to do that, especially people who are rather like you. However, the other half of the church needs to travel the journey with you. They can't leap to the conclusion, they need to follow your thinking and be with you on the journey, which is obvious to you, but not to them. We must explain the journey as well as the end point."

Raymond looked irritated. "Just tell me what you want me to do."

"OK" said Bruce, "I'll be as blunt as I can. You must take time with me as we consider the vision that God is giving us. I can then help people with the thinking behind the vision and you can concisely tell them what the vision is."

"Well why didn't you just say that in the beginning?"

Summary

Raymond doesn't Need a sensitive approach, and finds a diplomatic approach frustrating. He just Needs you to get to the point. Bruce is different - he does Need a sensitive approach to avoid him feeling hurt. Bluntness feels harsh to Bruce, whereas Raymond thrives on people being direct with him.

Raymond Needs to learn to be more sensitive with Bruce or Bruce will feel hurt and miss the message Raymond is giving. Bruce Needs to consider what he wants to say and try and condense it to a more focused point that Raymond can grasp. Once they understand their different Needs, they can adapt how they speak to one another and have a very successful relationship.

Who's in charge here?

The church youth group have looked at how they can engage with other activities in the town and have decided to set up a football team and a chess team.

Pastor Bruce meets with Ron and Barry, the two leadership interns, to ask them to take responsibility for these two new activities.

At the meeting, Ron leaps in with "I think I should lead the football team, the kids will need a clear leader, and they will listen to me. We'll be winning in no time."

Barry says nothing, so Bruce asks him what he thinks. Barry replies, "I don't mind. If Ron wants to be in charge that's ok."

Bruce has learnt that life is more complex than simply who is in charge. "I agree we want both of our teams to be winners, but we also want them to learn about teamwork and building relationships and be a good example by showing other teams that you can win with good sportsmanship and no foul play."

"Well, I can tell the football team that," Ron said. "I am sure they will do as they are told."

Barry thought a bit and then said "I can discuss that with my team – it's probably easier to achieve good sportsmanship with chess."

"I am interested that you seem to have agreed which teams you'll both lead," Bruce said. "I was thinking differently. The football team will need clear leadership, but also need to stick to the rules. So I was thinking they will need some very creative strategies to help give them an edge. Barry you're a very creative person, do you think you could help them to develop great strategy?" Barry said he would be very happy to do so and that he already had a number of ideas.

"I was also thinking about the Chess team," Bruce continued, "and how we can motivate them to win. I know that you can be really good at encouraging people Ron and wondered if you could think about how you would do that?"

Ron looked unhappy and said "So you want me to lead the Chess team and Barry the Football? Well that won't work, they will never listen to Barry and the football team needs clear strong leadership!"

Bruce half expected this response and said "I guess you've missed my point in your thinking there Ron. There is another way which I think may be stronger."

Summary

If they worked together, both leading both teams, then Ron's Need to lead and Barry's Need to include everyone, would really complement each other. But working together to lead both teams might not feel natural - they would need to understand and value each other's differences and make room for each other's Needs.

The rules are there for a reason!

Youssef and Graham have been asked to set up a Saturday early morning prayer group, to pray for their town and for the nation. They take turns in leading the group and have a good number of people attending.

After a few weeks it is clear that they are getting frustrated with each other.

Graham leads with a very open approach and anyone can be free to pray anything. He asks the Holy Spirit to come and the meeting goes off on all sorts of tangents.

Youssef Needs a structured approach with clear processes and procedures. He has a freshly prepared list each time and gives everyone a copy, so the group can pray for five minutes on each subject.

At the end of one of Graham's prayer meetings, Youssef lost it with Graham, "We can't go on like this, every time you lead its chaos! We have no idea where the meeting is going. We agreed a list of things we should pray for and I think we should stick to it. We always overrun when you're leading. "

Graham replied, "But you insist that there is only one way of running a prayer meeting, your way! I want to ensure there is space for God."

Summary

Youssef Needs clear structure and order in what he does. For him the rules are there for a reason, this risks giving no room for God's spontaneity. Graham, on the other hand, finds structure constraining, so he looks for variety in the things he does, but this risks never getting to the things God has actually asked him to do. Only by working together and valuing both perspectives, can you get the job done and create space for God to speak and act.

I win or we win?

Grace and Yinka are sisters who both enjoy swimming. A coach has noted that both of the girls are outstanding swimmers and approaches them to talk about joining the competitive swimming club. The coach describes the opportunities that would come by joining the club. Many members had won local and county events and some go on to compete at the Nationals.

Grace was very excited and enthusiastic. She really wanted to shine and now felt that the effort she'd been putting in was worth it. She and the coach talked through the different races she could train for. For Grace, the idea of competing to become the best in the club was very exciting.

Yinka was quiet. "What do you think Yinka?" asked the coach.

"I love swimming," replied Yinka, "but I was thinking of joining the water-polo team. Grace loves individual racing and beating others, but I think I could really add to the team and help them win, and I think that would be a lot of fun."

Summary

God made some of us more individually competitive than others, Grace loves to win and she works hard to get there, whilst Yinka finds being part of the winning team much more satisfying.

Individual sport like motor racing, needs a real star player – even though they are supported by a brilliant team. But having a star player in the football team might be a disaster – team sports need team-players. Context is everything; some competitions need a Grace to win the race and some need a Yinka to be a great team-player.

Getting competitiveness right in church can be a real struggle. Leadership must be a response to God's calling, not a response to our need to compete or our passion for the team. Is your desire to be a leader because God has raised you to lead or because you need to win and Church leadership 'looks' like winning? Or is your reluctance to lead because leadership "looks" like you're not part of the team?

Thinking about decisions

Following the resignation of William, the church administrator, Pastors Raymond and Bruce met to shortlist candidates.

When Bruce arrived, Raymond was already going through the applications. "I've been through them all," he said, "and Ruth meets all the requirements. I think she is the one. Have a read and make sure you're happy."

"Let's pray first. We need to listen to God to get this appointment right."

When they'd finished praying, Raymond said, "So what do you think of Ruth? I don't think you will find a better application."

"First, I am going to read them all, give me an hour and I'll have a better idea."

An hour later, Raymond returned. "Have you decided on Ruth?"

Bruce said, "Well I think we should seriously consider Ruth. But I also think Yasmin looks like a very organised person, and Geraldine seems to have some helpful communication experience. Bethany seems thoughtful and has some good ideas. So I think we should interview these four."

Raymond responded, "Well let's press on and get the interviews organised then, but we need to make a decision quickly, I don't want you to drag this out."

Summary

Raymond's decisiveness is powerful when a decision is needed. He is able to quickly filter information and come to a conclusion. If the decision was his alone, he would choose Ruth. When we don't think about it, we tend to choose people like ourselves.

Bruce Needs to think through all the nuances of an issue, taking time to get other people's ideas and gather maximum information. For Bruce, time spent considering all the aspects, is time well spent, as he will probably then make the best available decision.

If the Church had only one of these two Pastors it might suffer as a result of decisions biased by that Pastor's Personality. Raymond can easily make decisions that have not considered all the detail or the impact on other people or the future of the church. Bruce, on the other hand, can easily take so long praying and talking and considering every detail that he may not reach a decision at all. Together, when they remember and harness their differences, they can use both personalities and make very good decisions.

A clear focus on change

After selecting Yasmin as their new administrator, Raymond and Bruce were glad to see her start. She soon put efficient systems in place and established a clear structure to her week.

Yasmin knows where she is with Raymond, who is very busy and makes it clear just what he wants her to do. Bruce is also an efficient Pastor, but only puts effort where it is needed and she finds some of his ideas a bit impractical.

One day, Raymond entered Yasmin's office with some news. "We're starting work on the new kitchen soon, so we need Gail to share your office while the builders make the changes. Tell me if you two have any problems and I will find a fix."

Gail, the church evangelist, loved talking, so Yasmin was immediately anxious about sharing her office space.

Eventually Yasmin plucked up courage to speak with Bruce. She pulled out a piece of paper and read:

"Bruce, you need to know that I am really enjoying this job, but Raymond has told me that Gail will be sharing my office and to put it bluntly I am really concerned. I Need to be able to concentrate on one task at a time. I am pretty quick, but I Need to focus on the job in hand. I cannot see how I will be able to focus if Gail is talking all the time. I won't be able to do my job properly and you will think it is because I am not good at my job. You must find Gail somewhere else for her desk."

Bruce realised she was quite distressed and was somewhat surprised - she was normally a quiet sort. "Yasmin, it was certainly not our intention to upset you. We clearly didn't consider your needs in this. Let me talk with Gail. I am sure we can come up with a solution that protects how you work and enables you to stay focused."

Summary

Yasmin Needs to be able to focus on the task at hand, whereas Gail Needs plenty of variety. If sharing a room, Gail's Need to talk and her restlessness could easily affect Yasmin's productivity. Yasmin's Need to focus also means that surprises can be very damaging – she Needs time to understand the need for a change and to adapt to it.

This is where a compromise has to be made. Gail could move into the office with ground-rules that limit her social conversation to the first 10 minutes of the day and by making all phone calls in the Pastor's office. Future decisions like this Need to include Yasmin, to avoid such surprises!

Conform to tradition or freedom to be new?

Unlike the previous Needs, freedom does not have a colour and its measure is independent of the map.

Yvette is a pianist who reads music well and has done all her grades. She is a fairly quiet individual, but is reliable and never misses a music practice. Yvette might be called 'traditional' in her approach to music and worship - if a piano piece is written down, then that's how it should be played.

Gemma is a singer who loves every opportunity to shine; she always has a smile on her face and engages well with everyone in the team. She knows all the latest worship songs and loves having freedom to let go and see where the tune will take her.

Warwick has come to talk with the Worship Group about what God has been doing in the worship at his church. He talks about freedom and creativity as well as the need for accuracy and competency. "The music must not be a distraction from glorifying God". There is a lot of talk about 'waiting on God' and 'worshipping in the Spirit'.

When they break for coffee, Yvette is feeling very lost and wondering if she is part of the group at all. There seems to be no space for the hundreds of years of traditional music. "At least Gemma is enjoying herself," she thinks. "She is lapping it up; she will be dancing with flags again any time now! I just couldn't bring myself to do that."

After a break, Warwick asks if anyone has any questions. Yvette put her hand up: "Hi, I'm Yvette," she stammered. "All you have talked about this evening is freedom and creativity and going with the flow. You have not said one word about the value of our traditional hymns and songs, many of which speak such great truth. It is as if you don't care about anything that's more than a few months old. It's as if people like me don't have a place in the worship team."

Summary

Yvette's Need to conform to social tradition is easily met in those churches that hold on to a traditional style of church life. The danger is that the tradition can become so strong that it is possible to lose sight of what God is doing for today. Yvette risks being tempted into a legalistic tradition where the traditions can exclude God.

Gemma Needs independence and freedom. She will flourish in a church that is free to engage with God in the latest worship style. However, the danger here is no less, because such freedom means she too can lose sight of God and forget Him in her worship. She can be too busy just enjoying the emotional expressiveness of the latest worship songs. Gemma's Need for independence risks being tempted into self-centredness.

The key to worship is not a formula that meets Yvette's Needs or Gemma's Needs; It is creating a place where God can fill worship with life - a life that values historic truth as well as the creation of something new for today.

Do I Need a Challenge?

Winston, the architect, was working on some draft outline plans, when the new administrator, William, brought him the morning post.

"Hi William," Winston said. "You used to work with Raymond and Bruce. I was wondering which one is more important, which one should I try to keep happy. The new kitchen and café is rather a challenge – I'm trying to achieve all the different things they want, in a space which is not big enough, with a budget that is too small. One of them may have to accept some compromises and I was wondering who to approach?"

William said, "Well, they work as a team and although they are very different people, I don't think one is senior to the other. They take it that God is the 'Boss'. It sounds like quite a challenge to me. I'm sure you'll find a solution that works well."

Winston replied, "Not a problem. I love a good challenge and I have a bit of a reputation for taking on the difficult projects. Don't get me wrong, they're both great people, but as usual there is no obvious way to achieve everything they want."

Summary

Both men Need to succeed in their roles, but have very different perspectives when it comes to a challenge.

Winston Needs the challenge. He will take on all sorts of challenges and if they succeed, then that is great. If the challenge fails, he will of course be upset and may be quite hard on himself (and those people around him), but before long he will be ready for the next challenge.

William really Needs success, so will only take on a challenge after he's done all the research and can see how it will succeed. However, when things go wrong (which is rare because of his preparation), he will take that failure very personally and it can be quite some time before he is ready to take on another challenge.

Challenge has no colour in the Birkman map but this strong view of self, interacts with all of the Personality Needs, shaping every aspect of our Personality. When considering any of the above stories, by simply considering each character's Need for either High or Low challenge you can see how it will change the story.

What does this mean for me?

Now is a good time to re-visit the table in the last chapter and consider the guesses you made about your Needs.

Reflect on your role at church or at work and consider whether your roles, or those you relate to in those roles, meet your Needs.

If not, consider whether you can help people to meet your Needs by explaining your Needs to them.

If you feel that your role is so distant from your Needs that you are wondering if you should change role, then please consider getting a complete assessment of your Needs before making a drastic change. You could leap in entirely the wrong direction!

Focus on Needs in practice: -

Red corner: -	Things will work better for you if you help others to understand and adapt to your Needs.
Green corner: -	The lowest common denominator is not a good compromise. Harnessing differences means we can all win.
Blue corner: -	There are always other choices if we take time to consider the issues; creative solutions are not instant but are worth spending time on.
Yellow corner: -	You can build an effective team using a structured approach to understanding how people are different from you and how you can use those differences.
Central: -	Some people are a balance of each description, whereas others can have intensely strong Needs at one or the other end of the scale. Both are equally valid.

7

What do we mean by Strengths?

For we are God's handiwork, created in Christ Jesus to do good works, which God prepared in advance for us to do.

Ephesians. 2 v10

Now we dig much deeper into how complex people are, with a third perspective, which may be in a different place on the map from either your Interests or your Needs.

The idea of strengths is a positive and significant aspect of our culture. We are not talking here about physical or moral strengths, or even when we are strengthened by God's Spirit, but rather in terms of our Personality. Some people might even call such Strengths, your talents. What we mean by Strengths, are those aspects of us where we are effective or constructive, it is where we easily and confidently put our energy, and assuming that we express these Strengths most of the time, we would call them our 'Usual productive behaviour'.

We call it 'Usual' because there are times, such as when you are not well, or you are not getting your Needs met, that you do not perform so well. Of course, we all want success and so we strive to make our behaviour productive and constructive. While Strengths is a short and universally understood description, 'Usual productive behaviour' is a better name.

It is also important to retain a non-judgemental view about Strengths. For example, we either have a Strength, or we do not have that Strength. This is simply about difference. As soon as we adopt a language where the absence of a Strength is a weakness, then we quickly fall into a judgemental and unhelpful way of thinking.

The absence of a strength is not a weakness,

it is a difference

We indicate Strengths on the map with a diamond shape and we can plot our Usual-productive behaviour on the map in the same way we did with Interests and Needs. The language is similar, but of course the perspective will have changed.

Read each quadrant of the map and take a guess as to which colour resonates the most with your Strengths.

The Map of Strengths

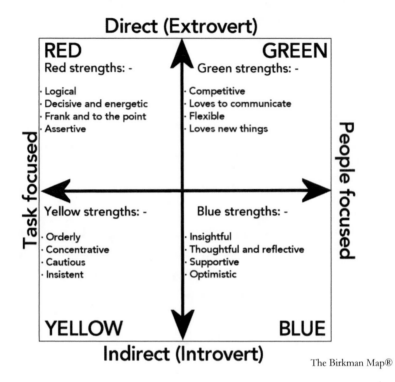

Direct (Extrovert)

RED
Red strengths: -

· Logical
· Decisive and energetic
· Frank and to the point
· Assertive

GREEN
Green strengths: -

· Competitive
· Loves to communicate
· Flexible
· Loves new things

Task focused

People focused

Yellow strengths: -

· Orderly
· Concentrative
· Cautious
· Insistent

Blue strengths: -

· Insightful
· Thoughtful and reflective
· Supportive
· Optimistic

YELLOW

BLUE

Indirect (Introvert)

The Birkman Map®

Four perspectives of Strengths

When we look at Personality Strengths, we discover that while we all have a uniquely different set of Strengths, we can see all of the Strengths reflected within God Himself.

Red Strengths

People with Red Strengths are active, decisive, assertive, enjoy being busy and are practical and forceful.

We see something of God's Red Strengths in His action of creation, (Genesis 1), with Noah and the flood (Genesis 7), with Moses and the plagues in Egypt (Exodus 8 to 11) and the decisiveness in the story of Jesus when a woman in the crowd touched His hem with faith and Jesus immediately stopped and asked "Who touched me?", He then brought healing to her (Matthew 9 v20). Jesus certainly was not subtle when He drove out the demons from the two possessed men (Matthew 8 v28). In the garden when Peter cut off the ear of the servant, Jesus stopped Peter and immediately healed the servant's ear (Luke 22 v50). Jesus was decisive and determined when He turned over the money lenders' tables; there was nothing subtle about what He did that day (Matthew 21 v12).

Green Strengths

We see that people with Green Strengths are communicative, competitive, flexible and enthusiastic about things that are new, and they can often be outspoken and independent.

God is communicative and makes Himself heard, He spoke the words into creation "Let there be light' and there was light (Genesis 1 v3). This can be seen throughout the Bible and especially when He speaks with Moses (Exodus 3 v14); Abraham (Genesis 13 v3); Isaac (Genesis 26 v2) and Jacob (Genesis 35 v9). He is the great "I am", yet Moses; Abraham and Hezekiah all argued with God and each time He showed His flexibility and changed His mind. When He created the world, He saw that it was new and good.

In Matthew 5 v39 Jesus teaches us to turn the other cheek, which is often interpreted as being anti-competitive. The truth is that this teaching is very competitive, because by turning the other cheek, He teaches us that through such love we can then win the person's heart. In John 15 v13 Jesus said, "Greater love has no one than this: to lay down one's life for one's friends". When Jesus laid down His life, He beat death itself and won new life for us all; what a great victory! What a win!

Blue Strengths

It is typical to find that people with Blue Strengths are insightful, thoughtful, reflective and optimistic, choosing a small group of close friends.

It is hard to argue that an omnipotent God is insightful or optimistic because God is perfect and knows the beginning from the end. Yet there is hope in the Passover and if the Israelites had trusted God they would not have spent forty years in the desert. Even though God knows the end of each story, He is in the story with us and He can be persuaded.

We see how God relates to insightfulness in that Jesus in his parables, which were made to be obscure, gave insight to His disciples (Matthew 13). God shows His thoughtful and reflective nature, when He appears to Elijah in the stillness. (1Kings.19 v12). Jesus asks us to consider how God clothes the lilies. (Luke 12. v27). He often sat and drew in the sand, or withdrew from the others to pray, even for 40 days in the desert.

The shortest verse in the Bible is where Jesus considers the reactions to Lazarus's death and 'Jesus wept', even though He already knew the end of the story. (John11 v35). Jesus had just 12 disciples, but there were three that appeared closest to Him (Matthew 17 v1). As for being an optimist, what can clearly be said is that Jesus through His death and resurrection is the embodiment of hope. We now all have hope for a future with God, so in giving us hope, He at least shows that He understands our optimism.

Yellow Strengths

We find that people with Yellow Strengths are orderly; concentrative, consistent, cautious and insistent.

God demonstrates His order and structure throughout the Old Testament. Through the Law, the Ten Commandments and through the rituals He instigated. Even though He knew we could never keep the Law, He wanted to demonstrate to all that this was true. He even inspired lists and genealogies, recognising the importance of the order of things. In Jesus, we see clear cause and effect structures, such as when He said, "Truly, truly, I say to you, unless one is born again he cannot see the kingdom of God" (John 3 v3). In Matthew 6 v33 He said, "But seek first the kingdom of God and His righteousness, and all these things will be added to you."

When He selected Luke to be one of His followers He chose a structured and ordered person who in his opening lines of his Gospel said, "Since I myself have carefully investigated everything from the beginning, I too decided to write an orderly account for you, most excellent Theophilus, so that you may know the certainty of the things you have been taught." Jesus also showed a degree of caution in that famous miracle at a wedding in Cana when He said to His mother "Woman, why do you involve me? My hour has not yet come." (John 2 v4).

Context

We said earlier that context is really important in shaping how we behave. It is also important when we consider the effectiveness of Strengths. The following is a thought exercise to designed to explore this further.

Imagine a Firefighter

Take a minute to think about the map above. Which colour Strengths do you think would make a good Firefighter? Red, Green, Blue or Yellow?

Do not read on until you have decided and made some notes as to why you have chosen the colour Strengths that you believe would make a good Firefighter.

Once you have decided on a colour, then read through the paragraph below that matches the colour you have chosen.

Does the paragraph match your reasons for choosing that colour?

Look back at the Strengths map on page 112. Which colour of the map best matches your Strengths?

Does your choice of colour for the Firefighter match your own Strengths colour?

If you chose the Firefighter with the same colour as your own Strengths, then you may have just had a glimpse of how your own perceptual filters colour the world you look at. If you have Red Strengths, you are likely to see the world as Red and are likely to make decisions based on that bias within you, that is, if you are Red then you are more likely to have chosen a Red Firefighter. Likewise if you are Blue yourself, you would more likely have chosen Blue. Most people tend to choose a firefighter of the same map colour that matches the colour of their own Strengths, but of course your own coloured perception may also cause you to say "I would not make a good firefighter" and therefore reject your colour as a result.

Is it really like that?

or is my perception colouring my thinking?

Knowing how you are biased can help you consciously keep check on your own views and help you to remember that other people are different from you. You might learn to ask when dealing with a problem, 'Is it really like that or is my perception colouring my thinking?'

Different colour Firefighters

RED

People with Red Strengths make good Firefighters, because they act quickly and are decisive, assertive and logical. They will get on with the task and do what needs to be done in order to put the fire out.

GREEN

Yet people with Green Strengths also make good Firefighters, because they are direct and want to beat the fire. They will communicate well to ensure the people are out of the building and will be flexible and adaptable in their approach to putting the fire out.

BLUE

Interestingly people with Blue Strengths make good Firefighters, because they can create a unique solution to each fire and can be very insightful especially when there is much confusion and ambiguity. They may simply tip the vase of water over the fire or create some other surprising solution, ensuring a good future for the people and the firefighters.

YELLOW

People with Yellow Strengths also make good Firefighters, because when dealing with a fire, they know there is a correct order to events and will methodically follow the plan as a member of the team. They will be really good at analysing data and refreshing policies and procedures to ensure every firefighter works with the maximum of efficiency.

Which is right?

There has been no study done to demonstrate the proportion of each colour group of people who are Firefighters. The above paragraphs show that anyone who is physically able, can be a good Firefighter and will bring to the role a different yet useful perspective.

It is reasonable to assume, that there are a higher proportion of Red people because it is likely to be attractive to them, the job having a considerable time in the outdoors and is task focused and technical /mechanical in nature. A fire is a very practical problem to fix. The role will also be attractive to Yellow people because it is a very structured, ordered and is a task-orientated role. Likewise, many Green people love to beat the fire and take any opportunity to talk with people. There are probably fewer Blue people who prefer to conserve energy but their creativity and strategic approach means that they may well find themselves managing other Firefighters. While there are probably more firefighters that are Red people, there is no correct answer.

Each Personality brings a different approach to the same context. One personality might be more effective than the next, don't assume your approach is the best

The power of collaboration

Remember Bruce, the Pastor at the local church? Imagine if he was on his own leading the church and he had just been given a large bequest to build a Café for the church and the local people. We know he is Blue and is therefore people focused, creative, reflective, thoughtful and conserves his energy. He turns to prayer easily as he wants to hear from God. Consequently, he will likely come to the project with lots of ideas about the look and the feel of the place and the atmosphere he wants to create.

He employs Winston the architect to develop the design and of course Winston knows that he must reach all the compliance requirements, so the kitchen will be safe and meet local standards. But Bruce won't be pushing for practicality and durability, so Winston will get the clear impression that it is the customer space that is important and any compromises Winston needs to make in order to meet the budget are likely to fall on the kitchen side. Decisions from Bruce will be hard to reach and the project is therefore likely to run behind time and when finished it will be beautiful but not necessarily practical.

Now let's consider what it would be like if Raymond was the only Pastor at the church. We know that Raymond is quite Red: direct and to the point, practical, pragmatic, perhaps even utilitarian in his approach to the task. The Café project is much more likely to have a practical and durable kitchen and the customer area is also likely to be very practical too. Winston would not get any impression that attention needs to be given to creating a particular atmosphere or style in the customer area, so it is likely to be straightforward and functional. Of course decisions will be easier for Winston and the project is very likely to be delivered on-time and on budget.

This is a good example of how any project will be lopsided if just one key person leads it. We saw from earlier stories that if Raymond and Bruce work together, then there is a better chance of creating a really good Café. If they were to extend their team and include Gail the

Green evangelist, then she would have brought a different perspective too, adding to the richness of the project. Gail could also have been helpful in getting people talking about the new opportunity and improving communication in general. If they had also added the new Yellow administrator Yasmin, then she could have documented ideas and decisions and helped by analysing the flow of people through the space for each different event. She may also have helped to develop a plan to deal with the need for temporary relocations during the building work, so would probably have found her own solution for Gail's office needs.

All projects exist in a state of tension between inclusive discussion and practical decisions. You can't include everyone; that would be far too complicated and messy and yet decisions made in isolation of people almost always end up having to be changed.

It is clear that if you have Strengths from all four quadrants; Blue creativity and ideas, Red practical implementation, Green communications and drive and Yellow planning, structure and order, then you stand a good chance of creating a rich, creative and practical project.

This is true of all collaborations, be it a project, a leadership team or worship group. The same principles apply.

Effective teams need to have input from and speak to,

all four colours of the map

Which Strength do you have?

These Strengths are made up of a number of components, that together crate your Strengths on the map

The table of Strengths below may look similar to one in an earlier chapter, but the context is of course changed. Here we are only thinking about your Personality Strengths, so before you look at the table, think about yourself when things are going well, imagine yourself at your most successful or productive, because that would be you behaving out of your Strengths.

While you can have Strengths at one side of the table or the other, or in the middle (that is a balance of both), you cannot have Strengths at both ends. When you read through the Strength descriptions below, think about your productive self and tick the box that best describes your Strengths when things are going well.

If you feel that both ends apply to you and neither side is particularly intense, then you may be a balance of both (tick the middle). However, if you feel both ends are intensely strong, then stop and think and look back at the Needs list you ticked in an earlier chapter, (page 86) because it is possible that you have developed an Unnatural Strength, that is, a Strength that is at the opposite end of the scale to your Need (more on this later). In this case, one side of the table is resonating with your Strength, while the opposite side is resonating with your Need.

Deliberately blank

Tick the side which best matches where you feel your Strengths are:-

Tick	Low Score	Balance of both	High Score	Tick
	Likes to work and think independently from the group.	Social Energy.	Enjoys teamwork and is comfortable in, and energised by, social settings.	
	Efficiently conserves energy balancing thought and action, reflective.	Physical Energy.	Is very active with high energy levels, is direct, forceful and immediate.	
	Is objective, practical and factual, focusing on immediate or end results. Prefers logic over feelings.	Emotional Energy.	Emotionally expressive and sympathetic, enjoying ideas and imagination, is comfortable with ambiguity.	
	Is frank, open and direct when dealing with others.	Self-consciousness.	Is serious, earnest, diplomatic and respectful when dealing with others.	
	Prefers to ask rather than tell, is self-directed and independent.	Assertiveness.	Is self-assertive and willing to defend a point. Enjoys being directed and directing others.	
	Is flexible and enjoys novelty and new methods of solving problems.	Insistence.	Likes details and creating, organising and using systems, rules or plans.	

Derived from the Birkman Method ®

Tick	Low Score	Balance of both	High Score	Tick
	Team-spirited preferring long-term gains benefiting all.	Incentives.	Is competitive and looks for tangible rewards for winning.	
	Grasps situations and evaluates them quickly, enabling quick decisions. Is objective and matter-of-fact.	Thought.	Is thoughtful and reflective considering all sides and possible consequences, draws on past experience and future impact before acting.	
	Is focused and concentrative and can sustain focus and resist distraction in order to complete.	Restlessness.	Enjoys a wide variety of tasks and will introduce additional tasks to maintain variety if needed.	
Not related to the map.				
	Conventional and traditional wanting to fit in with others. Is consistent and restrained.	Freedom.	Tends to be individualistic and not bound by convention enjoying new ideas and unusual situations.	
	Has reasonable view of what is achievable and is confident in their ability to achieve. Recovery from failure is hard.	Challenge	Seeks demanding challenges and is self-critical. Quickly recovers from failure.	

Derived from the Birkman Method ®

The average person is coloured by their perceptions

You may have found the exercise of putting ticks into the table quite difficult. This is in part because we are all coloured by our perceptions. If you found that you wanted to tick mainly in the middle, then you are simply reflecting your own view, that you are an average person, most people think they are average. One of the great strengths of the Birkman Method® assessment is that it really does measure your bias, demonstrating that you're not average. You can't really guess these things, but you will get some insight from this book.

Strengths in worship

Worship groups are a great example of how different people can work together. Worship is about giving glory to God and a corporate sharing of the experience of praising and worshiping through singing and other activities together. Some people will enjoy contributing to worship through dance and poetry, others through silence and again others just by singing - there are many different worship activities.

However, corporate worship usually has singing at the heart of it. As with the Café, if the worship is dominated by people from one colour quadrant, it can become lopsided and distorted. A worship team that has skilled musicians also needs to have people from all the quadrants of the map, to ensure that the Blue creativity is delivered with Red practicality and has Green communication with the people so that they are fully engaged. It also needs Yellow people with structure and order, to ensure a balance of traditional songs as well as new quality songs. This means that people can be led in an orderly way so that they stay engaged through the whole of the worship time.

I am not saying that worship is there to keep everyone happy, but it needs to lead all those present into engagement with worshiping God. If worship leaders take account of the wide range of Needs and use the different Strengths available, then they can ensure that everyone can worship God and hear from Him. Using the simple approach of the four colours of the map helps to ensure that we don't simply get trapped in our own one or two colours.

Colour traps

One important principle that we have not yet explored, is the fact that we like people who are similar to ourselves.

This frequently leads to a trap. Because we like people who are like ourselves and understand us well, we find them easy to work with and we tend to gather such people around us. This can happen in any team, from the Board Room to the coffee room. I have watched senior executives appoint their senior team with people who are just like them. This is not simply appointing 'yes-men' which is a related but different problem, this is much more subtle and ultimately more damaging as it constrains and limits the team.

We like people who are like ourselves,

so we can easily build biased teams

Imagine you have a committee aimed at supporting a group of people in your community, they could be refugees or the elderly, for example.

Now imagine you have appointed a Chairperson who is quite Red. They will be direct, decisive and action orientated. If the Chairperson is not self-aware, they will tend to appoint other Red people around them, because their perceptual filter colours their world Red and Red people are the most like-minded to them. Now you can imagine such a committee of Red people would definitely be a powerhouse for getting things done, but of course all this Red-behaviour reinforces itself as the best way, or even the only way, for getting things done.

Now if a Green or Yellow person is a member of that team, they may find the committee can be a little difficult. Their Personality style is not so far from the Red, so they may well adapt and cope.

A Blue person may find it very difficult indeed if they don't understand what is going on. For example, imagine you're a Blue person appointed to that committee. You may feel that everything is very directive, short and to the point, that there is little opportunity to express your more creative ideas and thoughts and consequently you might struggle to be part of the committee.

However, if you do understand that all this directness is the committee simply being Red, then it can become easier to speak into the bluster. You can establish the common purpose that the group is there for and that each person has a different and valuable perspective, making it clear that by bringing together all the thinking, the Red committee will make better decisions and actions. Now you have a way of working with the Reds.

Imagine a Green person leading a youth group. If they are not self-aware, they are likely to gather leaders around them who are also very Green. Because of their perception bias, they may feel that their way of doing things is the right or only way of doing things and therefore present to the group that they should be behaving in this particular Green way. While the Red and Blue people may understand something of the Green person's style, a Yellow person may find it completely demoralising as they have little hope of success, because they were not made like that. A Yellow person is likely to withdraw from such a youth group and you will end up with a group that is biased towards the dominate colour, in this case Green.

How the team uses all the colours

Follow the productive journey of any group or team when they use all the colours of the map as shown in this example: -

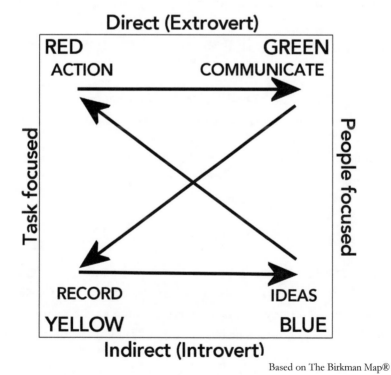

Based on The Birkman Map®

- A Blue person creates a new idea.
- Then a Red person makes it happen.
- Next a Green person tells everyone about it.
- Finally, a Yellow person records what happens and tells the Blue person what worked and what didn't.
- Then the Blue person adapts their original idea to make it better.
- The Red person makes the changes happen.
- And so on round the cycle......

If there is a perspective missing then the work will not flow well round the team.

Missing Red?   = Lots of ideas and talk yet nothing gets done.

Missing Green?   = Great work is done yet no-one gets to know about it.

Missing Blue?   = Loads of work is done yet next week it will be done again.

Missing Yellow? = Great work is done, but no-one knows how many or how much or if it should it be done again.

Whatever colour Strengths you have in yourself and in your team, you can only avoid it being a lopsided team, by either consciously filling the gap by adapting your behaviour, or adding to the team someone who God designed with different strengths than can fill the gap for you.

Mountains, perspectives and leadership in the Church

In the late 1970's, I was part of a small fellowship in Hastings when we had the joy of a visiting speaker. During the meeting, he brought a prophetic word about how the leadership was to be in the church. I paraphrase it now, as his words were not recorded, but he said: -

"I see a range of mountains with several peaks. God drew my attention to one peak that was clearly the highest and I felt God say, 'see this one, he is the leader'. He then led me around the base of the mountain until I could see the range again. I could still clearly see the peak that He had drawn my attention to earlier, yet from this new perspective I could now see it was not the tallest. In fact it was clear that a different peak was the tallest. He then led me to a different vantage point where I could hardly see the first peak and yet now I could see a third peak that was taller than the second. He then led me further to a fourth peak and now from this perspective it was the tallest.

Each time I changed my perspective I could see that a different peak was now the tallest, so who was the leader? God said to me 'This is how the church leadership is to be. No one is meant to be the tallest, except when I prompt them to take the lead for a particular task or time.'

This picture of a range of mountains where different peaks become more prominent depending on the different perspective, speaks very clearly into the way church leadership should function. It brings together the five-fold ministries, as described by Paul in Ephesians. 4 v11, along with each of the four colour perspectives, into a team where each person honours, values and promotes the others, to God's glory.

God gives gifts, be that Apostle; Prophet, Evangelist, Pastor or Teacher. Yet He also gave each one a Personality that brings different Strengths. That enables the team to glorify God as He intends and to build the church and bless the people. God wants all the gifts He gives, to work together.

High Interests and Usual Behaviour together make our Strengths

As well as our Usual productive behaviour, we can also find that our high scoring Interests can also be considered as Strengths, because they energise us so we are quick to put our energy it to these areas.

When you add elements of Interests and Usual behaviour together, you can start to see more of how these Personality differences shape how we behave and colour our thinking. If you met me and witnessed my Usual productive behaviour, you would say that I am an extrovert. However, I also have a high 'Technical / Mechanical' Interest, I like to make things work. Together you can see in me a person who is usually not shy and likes to be very solution orientated. Even the way I am writing this book, is driven to ensure you gain enough insight to make a difference in your life. If you read this book and nothing changes, I would feel a failure, but I work hard at the text to try and ensure it will make a difference to you, that is, that the book will work. Boldly fixing problems is part of my Strength.

When I play bass guitar I am very conscious of the emotions that music creates. I don't look simply at the logic of the notes on the musical score, I am much more Interested in the feel of the groove, as my high 'Emotional Energy' Usual score combines with my high 'Musical' Interest score. My children used to complain that I made them sit through the credits at the end of a film at the cinema. I would explain that someone went to great lengths to shape the music to feed out the end of the film in a particular way and that was part of the emotional engagement with the film itself. This is part of my Strength.

When you talk with me about an issue or problem, then you will find I ask lots of questions, because 'I Need to understand', this is shown by my strong 'scientific Interest' score. Combined with my extrovert Usual and high technical/mechanical Interest scores, you will find that I can keep on asking 'why, why, why?' and drilling right down to the root of an issue because I want to solve the problem. This combination is a real strength in me, I keep pressing on till I have evaporated all the assumptions and helped to find the real root of the issue and potential solution.

Focus on Strengths: -

Red corner: -	People with Red Strengths get things done, but they get the right things done when they work together with the other colours, especially with Blue people.
Green corner: -	People with Green Strengths, communicate really well, but they give the right message when they work with the team and especially with Yellow people.
Blue corner: -	People with Blue Strengths create ideas and strategy, but these ideas only become practical with the help of the rest of the colours, especially Red people who can make things happen.
Yellow corner: -	People with Yellow Strengths record and organise information that can inform ideas and their practical application. They will only record the right information, when others tell them, especially Green people who talk to many people.
Central: -	Central people can understand the importance of each of the four perspectives, but they need people who have more extreme perspectives to avoid missing the best and more radical solutions.

8

The Strengths God gives us and the Strengths we learn

Every good and perfect gift is from above, coming down from the Father of the heavenly lights, who does not change like shifting shadows.

James. 1 v17

By Personality Strengths, we mean the unique set of behaviours that other people consider that you are good at. You may also have some latent Strengths that have never been explored by you and therefore remain hidden from other people.

Our Strengths are a combination of our Usual-productive behaviour along with our most energising Interests.

In the last chapter, we described our Usual productive behaviour, which uses the same named areas; Social Energy, Physical Energy etc., as for our Needs. However, we looked at these areas from this very different perspective.

Now we need to ask how our Needs and Usual behaviour relate to each other. Do our Strengths reflect our Needs? Are they the same or different and if different why?

Consider my Needs for a moment; we saw in chapter 5 that my Needs are in the bottom right of the map, in the Blue quadrant, quite some distance from my Interests that are in the top left, that is, the Red area.

Even if you know my Interests and Needs, you can't guess where Usual behaviour will appear - although you might guess it is somewhere between the two, this isn't usually the case. As it happens, my Usual behaviour score *is* between my Interests and Needs, but this is unusual. Look at the map below and you will see my Usual behaviour expressed as a diamond on the map.

The Authors map

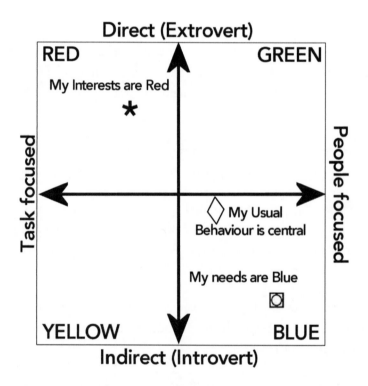

The Birkman Map®

While knowing that my Usual behaviour is fairly central gives me some insight into my Personality, it tells me nothing of the relationship between Usual behaviour and Needs.

If you got to know me, you would know that I have a high Need for feelings first (Emotional Energy), rather than logic. I Need opportunity to talk about how I am feeling about something. When things go wrong I want to talk about how I am hurt or upset. I Need to have opportunity to express my emotions.

At the same time, I am very comfortable talking with someone about their emotions and people find it easy to open up to me. My Usual behaviour is to think about how someone feels before thinking about the logic of a situation.

So, when it comes to Emotional Energy, you can see that my Usual productive behaviour matches my Need - they are both 'high' scores. I have developed a Strength that matches my Need. While we know the Need is God given, I have developed a Strength that matches that Need.

If I had developed a Usual behaviour at the bottom of the Emotional Energy scale, you would observe that my Usual behaviour, my Strength, was to be logical and un-emotional. Then my Strength would not match my Need.

Understanding this relationship between your Need and your Strength is important because of a common behaviour that we all subconsciously have, that is we tend to mirror people that we like.

Mirrors

We generally treat other people in the way we feel is appropriate, this is usually based on the way we see them behave. If someone that we want to get on with is very chatty, we tend to mirror their behaviour and are then chatty back to them. Likewise, if someone is more reserved, then again, we tend to mirror what we see and are less chatty back.

This is most obviously true with body language. When two people are trying to be friends, they can easily mirror their physical positions, if one crosses their leg then the other will unconsciously do the same very soon after. You can see some great examples of this if you search the web for images of 'politicians mirroring'. But does this mirroring approach work? Well some of the time yes it does and other times it fails completely.

When we are trying to get on with someone,

we tend to reflect back or 'mirror' their behaviour

Reflected Usual Behaviour might meet my Need

Remember that when thinking about my Emotional Energy, what you would see in my Usual behaviour is a person who is obviously comfortable with talking about feelings. You might almost say that my obvious comfort in this area would give you permission to talk about how you are feeling.

Therefore, you are likely to reflect back to me my Usual behaviour, you are likely to be as comfortable with emotional matters with me, as you can be.

Consequently, your reflected behaviour meets my Need for opportunity to talk about my feelings.

This is why I call this a God-given Strength. While God gave me the Need when He shaped my Personality, I also learned to be strong in the same area to match that Need. Such matching works well and is positive and healthy, simply because the consequence of my behaviour, is that you are likely to naturally meet my Need.

A God-given Strength will naturally meet my Need

Unnatural Strengths

However, as we grow and are influenced by those around us we can find their pressure, shapes our Usual behaviour to be different from our Need, even the opposite from what we Need from others.

For example, I am very focussed, organised and meticulous in my planning, which is shown in my high Insistence score in my Usual behaviour. I have learned to be very comfortable with the detail.

Therefore, when you observe my comfort with detail and plans, you are likely to reflect back to me, what you have observed. For example, you are likely to give me or even impose on me a definite plan with detailed instructions, rules and procedures.

And if you behaved that way towards me, rather than meeting my Need, you would very quickly drive me crazy, because my Strength in detail is learned and does not match my God-given Need at all, in fact it is the opposite of my Need.

This is why I call this an Unnatural Strength rather than a God-given Strength. God made me to Need just a broad outline to follow, with loads of variety and the most minimal amount of routine. My Need is not like my Strength.

An unnatural Strength will not meet my Need

Now we know that if my Need is not met over a long period of time, the internal stress that this will cause in me, will eventually erupt in stress-behaviour, a destructive attempt at getting my Need met. If you keep treating me in the way you see me, then at some point you are likely to see me erupt quite unhelpfully and you will not know why.

Example of my unnatural Strengths at work

You now know that I have learned to be quite structured and ordered. Some years ago, I was responsible for building a stage and storage rooms and installing a new Sound System for my church. I knew that a clear plan would really help to ensure that the stage and sound system would work in the way we all wanted it to. I had no problem creating a clear plan for the contractors and fully expected them to deliver everything according to the plan and I would hold them to it. The Church leader who oversaw the project had trusted me to come up with the plan and let me get on with it, so it was all good.

Some way through the project, the responsibility changed and the new leader wanted to micro-manage me and kept trying to tell me how the plan should be. You also know that I do not have a high Insistence Need, that is, I Need a simple outline or broad plan rather than an intricate one.

My Need is very different from how I usually behave. The consequence of this new leader constantly trying to 'Interfere with my plan' (which is how I saw it), was very stressful and the tensions grew worse each week, which led me to become quite disorganised and this disorganisation on my part (which was an unhelpful attempt to get my Need for flexibility met), led the leader to try harder to impose his plan on me. Which made my frustration worse and so the cycle continued; it was not fun!

The new Leader saw that I was usually structured and ordered and therefore reflected that behaviour to me, believing that was what I Needed. Of course, I did not Need that and the stress behaviour that grew in me was dreadful. While I am not proud of my behaviour back then, I now understand what was going on and why the leader's genuine attempts at being helpful caused me such problems. If I were in the same position today I would have been able to explain that I did not perform well when 'micro-managed' and would have checked carefully with him to ensure that I understood all the issues that were important to him and then asked him to let me get on with it.

My unnatural Social Energy Strengths

These learned Strengths are not bad in and of themselves, but because they do not help us to get our Needs met, we have to learn how to manage them to avoid the destructive stress-behaviour.

For example, the measure of my Usual behaviour for 'Social Energy' is high, that is, I am usually really good in a group or at a social occasion. I have no hesitation when I stand up in front of hundreds of people to speak at a seminar or at some other meeting. So if you saw me in those contexts you would say I have a Strength there, probably describing me as an extrovert.

However, when it comes to my Needs, my 'Social Energy' score is relatively low, which means I Need time alone to digest and think things through. At the end of a big meeting I do not want to go out and chat with loads of people, because I have already been drained by this social activity (you might be energised by it, we are all different). I now Need time to recharge my batteries and for me, that means time alone. At such times you would definitely consider me an 'Introvert'. That is when I definitely behave as the introvert God made me to be.

I have learned through my formative years that behaving as an extrovert is a successful behaviour for me, so I have developed this 'unnatural' Strength. But it comes with a flaw, in that when I become tired by the behaviour, I run away and this can cause confusion to others. Those people who have me pegged as an extrovert wonder what on earth is going on when I become that natural introvert.

Risk of stress behaviour

So God-given Strengths, help us to get our Needs met and reduces the risk of seeing stress-behaviour. Whereas Unnatural Strengths, while just as useful in themselves, do not help us to get our Needs met and therefore increase the likelihood of counterproductive stress behaviour suddenly appearing.

Most people have a mixture of both natural and unnatural Strengths.

The key to understanding what is going on in you as an individual, is through understanding, so that you can then adapt how you behave, to both be true to your Strengths, while also ensuring that your Needs are met.

Unnatural and God-given Strengths at work in a relationship

Rachel and Paul, a couple who have been married for many years, have differing Needs and Strengths in 'Self-consciousness', that is, in one to one relationships.

When it comes to one to one communication, Rachel has both Red Needs and Red Strengths. Her Strengths match her Needs, so they are 'God given or natural Strengths'. She is very direct when she speaks to you and she Needs you to be direct back to her. No padding, no frills, she just gets to the point - and Needs you to do the same.

Paul however, although he has Red Needs like Rachel, has learnt to be very diplomatic and subtle with his words. He has learnt to behave with Blue Strengths. His 'Unnatural Strengths' do not match his Need.

When Rachel speaks to Paul she is direct and to the point, which is just what Paul Needs. That means she communicates effectively, without the risk of prompting stress-behaviour in Paul.

However, when Paul communicates with his Blue Strengths, he is subtle, diplomatic and wraps up issues with a good deal of sensitivity. Rachel finds this very irritating - she just Needs Paul to get to the point, his 'dithering' can cause her to snap back with frustration. In all their communication, it is Paul who gets the blunt frustration back from his diplomatic attempts and it can feel very discouraging.

Today, Paul understands what is going on. He now thinks through what he needs to say, boils it down and tries to stick to communicating the essentials to Rachel. It is not easy for him to do this, because it is hard to change his behaviour from the indirect unnatural Strength he has learnt and developed, but his communication is much better than it was.

Their communication styles affect other relationships too. When Rachel meets a stranger, she is quite direct with them and so they tend to mirror her directness back to her. Because her 'Natural Strength' meets her Need, there is no confusion, so communication is generally successful, although somewhat short.

When Paul meets a stranger, he is sensitive, diplomatic and subtle (which he has learned is an effective strategy) and so other people tend to be polite and subtle back, which of course does not meet Paul's Need.

There is no way for others to know this, therefore communication can be much more difficult with Paul. Because his 'Unnatural Strength' is so different from his Need there is much more opportunity for confusion.

Now Rachel and Paul have a fuller understanding of their personalities, they are both better equipped to articulate their Personality and Needs. Communication is therefore much better for them both. Understanding your unique Personality and then being able to articulate it to others makes life much easier and much healthier.

Understanding why we are different from ourselves

This discrepancy between a learnt behaviour Strength and a different God-given Need is why many personality assessments don't feel as if they reflect your Personality correctly.

They assess the Strengths that you have, but if that Strength does not match your Need, then you will know that the assessment doesn't fully speak to the individual that you are. It may also account for why some assessments show that a repeated test can give a very different report. On one occasion your Strengths come to the front and on another, your Needs are more prominent, giving you a different result.

Some people find their Needs and Strengths are very close to each other, while others find their Strengths are the furthest distance possible away from their Needs on the map.

This is why guessing a person's Personality, is both at times very helpful and at other times potentially dangerous, especially when you assume too much!

Are unnatural Strengths hypocritical?

Is it hypocritical to behave in one way when our Needs would prefer us to behave differently? 'Do as I say not as I do' is a very old saying and may go back to Jesus who said of the Pharisees,

"But do not do what they do, for they do not practice what they preach".

Matthew. 23 v3

The key here is to look at motivation or intention. The Pharisees abused their power and their position for their own gain, whereas we can adapt our behaviour to do what is effective for the best of reasons.

If our learned behaviour does not meet our Needs, we are always at risk of being tripped up - especially if we don't have the opportunity to explain this difference between how others see us and the Personality God has given us.

The Golden Rule is overtaken

Philosophy has seen the Golden Rule established for centuries

"Treat others as you Need to be treated".

But this can now be superseded by Dr Birkman's Platinum Rule,

"Treat others in the way that *they* Need to be treated".

This can only be achieved if either: -

1. The other person has developed natural Strengths that align to their Needs, so that when we reflect back the behaviour we see, their Needs are met.

or

2. The other person can tell you what their Needs are, so that you can adapt your behaviour and respond more appropriately to what they Need.

How much can you adapt?

If your Strengths are very introverted, then no matter how hard you try, it is very difficult to adapt your Strengths to behave at the opposite end of the scale. Behaving in a very direct way as an extrovert is a leap too far for most introverted people.

Most adults past their mid-20's can reasonably adapt their behaviour by a maximum of about 30% difference. If your Strength in communication is very indirect, let's say right at the bottom of the map, then there is little point telling you that you should be an extrovert. No matter how hard you try, you wouldn't even reach the midpoint. You can be a great actor, but it will be an act. Likewise, it would be pointless for an Extrovert at the top of the map to try to adapt their behaviour to be an introvert - the transition is just too great.

But here's the good news: even if the best that two opposite people can achieve is to move up to 30% closer to one another, two people both moving 30% is a 60% reduction in the gap which is a very significant change!

Clarification about Personality being fixed

You may be asking the question, "Did the author not say earlier that Personality is fixed and can't be moved?"

For Interests and Needs this is true, they do not change. It is hard to prove this, as children have not developed the language to enable them to be assessed, but most experts would agree that adult Needs and Interests either are, or have become, fixed, by their mid-twenties and do not change over the rest of their life. It was clearly Dr Birkman's opinion, that they are God given and persistent throughout the whole of life.

Strengths are more flexible because we adapt them as we learn. By our mid-twenties, they are stickier and harder to change; hence they can only be changed by up to 30%. But with God, all things are possible, so it may be that with His help we can adapt Strengths further. There is just no study that shows what God can do in people when through prayer and the power of the Holy Spirit, God breaks into a person's life.

How Unnatural Strengths can shape our whole life

Let me introduce you to Gavin Brown, whom we employed as a salesman. Gavin had been in Information Technology sales for over

30. Naturally I insisted that we would understand him better if I went through an assessment with him.

Once completed, we arranged to talk through his profile and could see it was not going to be a straightforward conversation. I called Gavin and before we got very far into the discussion, he said "I guess you're going to tell me that I am not really a salesman? I think I'd better be honest with you from the outset. When I was at school, I really wanted a great car, a fast car that would attract the girls. I looked around at what people drove and I saw that salesman always got good cars. I am afraid that was the basis of my career choice."

Gavin had Blue Interests which he had largely ignored. He also had Red Needs which did come through his sales style to some degree. He had very Green Strengths because he had learnt to be a salesman, driven by his decision about cars. Once he started on the journey of sales he became quite good at it and made a career that did not reflect his natural Needs and Interests.

Having 'Unnatural Strengths' does not mean that you will not be successful. In fact, sometimes you can be more successful because of your unnatural Strengths. Gavin was not a typical salesman, because his Strengths were so different from his Needs and Interests and that meant he was a more complex salesman than most. Gavin saw opportunities that the typical salesman might miss. However, Gavin also knew that sales and the typical sales approach were not satisfying for him.

Today he is still a salesman but his approach has embraced his underlying Blue Personality that he had been trying to ignore. For Gavin, the world is much more open now (and he has even bought a guitar, reflecting his undeveloped Musical Interests).

Focus on Strengths and Needs: -

Red corner: -	People understand you when your Strengths match your Needs, but can be easily confused when they do not.
Green corner: -	There is a real advantage to you if your Strengths can move closer to your Needs as people will understand you better.
Blue corner: -	Understanding how your Strengths do or do not match your Needs, can enable you to develop strategies to help ensure your Needs are met and you minimise stress behaviour.
Yellow corner: -	While understanding Strengths and Needs is complex, it is logical and orderly and therefore quite understandable.
Central: -	When Strengths and Needs are close, it is easier to understand, when the gap is more extreme, it is much harder to understand.

9

Learning to love the Personality that God gave you

You, my brothers and sisters, were called to be free. But do not use your freedom to indulge the flesh; rather, serve one another humbly in love. For the entire law is fulfilled in keeping this one command: "Love your neighbour as yourself."

Galatians. 5 v13-14

Loving my neighbour as myself – it's a tall order. Many of us find this difficult and not just because we are called to love our neighbours. For some of us, the real sticking point is that to love others well, we must love ourselves well. It is not enough to understand your unique Personality, you also Need to accept it, value it, delight in it, honour it, give thanks for it and work with it.

Hopefully, working through this book has given you some insight into your unique Personality. You've discovered Interests that either energise or drain you (Chapter 4) and Needs that God gave you when he made you (Chapters 5 and 6). Chapter 7 helped you understand how your Strengths may be close to or distant from your Needs. Chapter 8 talked about how our God-given Strengths flow from our Needs, whilst acknowledging that learnt behaviours are effective but draining, so we will need time to recover and there is a risk of stress behaviour.

Each time you ticked a Need or Strength box, not only were you declaring that you are similar to that statement, you were also agreeing that you are different from the opposite statement. In the process of accepting that you are a unique individual, you are also agreeing that other people are not like you. Some are similar, others different to some extent and some will be so far off your radar that you will have to work hard to understand them. You may never fully understand people who are at the extreme opposite to you, but with awareness, you can adapt your behaviour in order to have better conversations, more effective worship, more engaging times of prayer and have the Word of God speak into your life.

How to engage with, accept and love your God-given Personality

The following is summarised in a work sheet in Appendix 2, in order that later, you can work through this yourself.

Thank God

The starting place is to thank God for the Personality He has given you. Thank Him for the energising Interests and consider how they are, or could be, working in your life. Then give thanks for your God-given Needs and Strengths, especially where your Strengths naturally match your Needs.

Ask God

Ask God to speak with you about your learnt Strengths. Recognise that while they may be successful, they will not meet your Needs. Seek God's help in allowing you, where you can, to relax back towards your more natural Strengths that will meet your God-given Needs.

A good next step would be to ask God to show you opportunities to put your energy into the top Interests and natural Strengths God has given you.

You may also ask Him to show you how to let go of roles that will drain you dry, however, if you have no choice but to undertake such a role, you should try to complement it with an Interest that energises you.

Finally ask God to help you understand the individuals around you so that you can help them to be their best, for God's Glory.

Know your limits and Needs

Be honest about your Needs. Let people know what you Need, so that they have the opportunity to adapt their behaviour to better meet your Needs. They may want you to shine, but are blinded by their own perceptual filters. So tell them lovingly and gently, how God made you to Need certain things that may be different from them.

If God presents you with a person in need, in the way He did with the Good Samaritan, do your best in that moment. Know when you have done enough and pass the matter on to someone else who is better designed to deal with the issue (unless of course God made you to be that person who can help).

It's Ok to be Human

Being forgetful is part of life, so if other people forget your Needs then tell them again, because other people will default to their own Strengths and forget what you Need.

Being forgetful is not a sin; it is a reality of life that grows with age.

Don't be hard on yourself, if past decisions turn out to be a bad match for your Personality. Parents, teachers, advisors and society, generally do not know what is best for you, but they usually do try the as hard as they can.

Whether your Strengths are natural or developed through what you have learnt, then delight in them.

How to undertake this approach

Use the structured approach in Appendix 2, as a foundation for the practice of loving your Personality.

There is no right or wrong way to approach using this, but here are some different ways a person from each colour might: -

- If you are Red, then just do the things in the list.

- If you are Green, talk about this list and complete it in the order you feel is best.

- If you are Blue, then use this list to inspire you to create your own approach.

- If you are Yellow, then work through everything on the list carefully.

A practical example

In order to give you a flavour of how to work through, this approach to accepting and loving yourself, I thought it might help you explore this from my perspective Therefore, I have written my own response below.

First you need to know me better, so these are my areas of Interests:-

	Score	Comments.
• Musical.	10	These are my High Interests that are energising.
• Technical /Mechanical.	9	
• Scientific.	8	
• Artistic.	7	These are neither high nor low so are less significant to me.
• Outdoor.	6	
• Social Service.	5	
• Numerical.	4	
• Persuasive.	3	
• Literary.	2	These I find draining and I should do my best to avoid.
• Administrative.	1	

Derived from The Birkman Method®

You will see that I have three High Interest scores. When I put energy and effort into these types of activities, they always energise me more.

I am biased towards these three, in that the first thing I want to do when something doesn't sound right (Musical) is to understand it (Scientific) and then fix it (Technical/Mechanical). In fact music, which relates to all sounds, is so important that I Need such Interests in my life in order to have some satisfaction.

You will also see that my two lowest scores are Literary and Administrative. Therefore, undertaking activities that require these Interests is very draining to me and best avoided. As I am writing this book I have to counter the draining effect by using other activities to help maintain my energy levels.

Before I run through my personal response, look at my Needs and my Strengths in the table below. You will see that I have only included the statements that are relevant to me. Some are a balance of both so you need to read the left and the right statements and remember that neither is intense, so in those cases they both speak some truth about me.

Over the page you will see my table:-

- The table shows my Needs as Circles: - **O**

- My Natural Strengths that meet my Needs are shown as Diamonds as: - **N◊**

- My learnt or Unnatural Strengths that don't meet my Needs are shown as: -**U◊**

	Low Score	Balance of both	High Score	
O	Does not Need to be part of group preferring time alone.	Social Energy.		
			Is usually sociable and outgoing.	U◊
	Needs to conserve energy reflecting on ideas at own pace. Usually conserves energy efficiently balancing thought and action.	O Physical Energy N◊ (Balance Both)	Needs to be active with practical results and physical action. Usually is very active with high energy levels, is direct, forceful and immediate.	
		Emotional Energy	Needs feelings, thoughts and close relationships in which to confide.	O
			Is usually emotionally expressive, sympathetic and imaginative.	N◊
U◊	Is usually frank with people.	Self-consciousness	Needs a diplomatic approach.	O
	Needs autonomy and easy relationships.	O Assertiveness	Needs to know who is in charge and can be in charge if no one else is.	
			Is usually self-assertive and willing to defend a point. Enjoys directing others.	U◊
O	Needs a simple outline plan only.	Insistence		
			Is usually very organised and detailed.	U◊

Derived from The Birkman Method®

	Low Score	Balance of both	High Score	
		Incentives	Needs to compete and to win, with clear rules to competition.	O
U◊	Is usually Team-spirited preferring long term gains benefiting all.			
		Thought	Needs time to think; digest ideas and to consider and reflect before action.	O
	Usually grasps situations and evaluates quickly, decisive and objective.	U◊	Is usually thoughtful and reflective considering all sides before acting.	
		Restlessness	Needs a variety of tasks, frequent changes and flexible routines.	O
U◊	Is usually focused and concentrative and resists distraction so can complete.			
		Not related to the map.		
		Freedom	Needs freedom from social constraints and outside control.	O
			Usually tends to be individualistic and not bound by convention enjoying new ideas and unusual situations.	N◊
O	Needs achievable success and public approval.	**Challenge**		
N◊	Usually has a reasonable view of what is achievable and confidently can be achieved. Recovery from failure is hard.		*Derived from The Birkman Method®*	

© Colin Shewry 2017 | Page 159

As you read my responses in the description below of how to engage with, accept and love your God-given Personality, you may need to refer back to these tables to understand where my Needs and Strengths are.

Author's response: -

Thanking God for my Personality

It can be hard to appreciate our own Personality, especially when we are aware of our limitations, but God created us entirely as He intended. For many years I did not recognise the unique elements that God placed in me and even when I sort of knew, I could not articulate it. I can now explain myself much better and embrace my unique Personality. I can explain to others how they can get the best from me and how I can adapt my behaviour to get the best from them.

Coming to recognise my Interests means I can respond to them in a way that energises rather than drains me. For example, my high Scientific score means I really do *Need* to understand and will ask people "why?" many times to drive out their assumptions and get to the heart of the issue. Then there are the less helpful ways I can respond to my high scores - my high technical/mechanical score means I have to be careful not to leap into solving problems that are not my responsibility, even if I am drawn to them. Recognising low scores is just as important – my low literary score informed me that to write this book I would need all sorts of help from other people.

Knowing that we have areas of natural Strength which also meet our Needs means we can relax and enjoy our Personality. I have never felt the need to conform to others' expectations; this is reflected in my freedom score and has helped my creativity. I am also very comfortable showing and working with emotions - crying has never bothered me and I am very comfortable when others open up about how they really feel.

Likewise, understanding that our Strengths are different from anyone else's gives us freedom. I have never been very active, but I no longer have to feel guilty about it because I now know this was not in my design. I have always been a little more reflective and thoughtful than most people, but now I know I *Need* time to think things through before making a decision. When stressed I can become very authoritarian, but knowing that, means I have learnt to watch out for it and to guard against it.

Whilst I still believe that collaboration is the best way to get things done, I also recognise my competitiveness and don't feel embarrassed by winning games - even though my children hate it! I am still very comfortable with a crowd and find talking with hundreds of people easy. However, I now no longer feel guilty about giving myself time alone or time with just one or two trusted friends.

When talking with others I know that I can be rather direct yet I have always known that it hurts me to get such directness back. I am still working on getting this right.

Recognising these things shows us where we might have difficulty, but that's ok.

Thanking God for all aspects of our Personality can be hard – especially when we have discovered things about ourselves that we might not like. But when we realise that God has designed us exactly as He wants us, we can come before Him and praise Him for what He has given us.

My prayer

> *I thank you, Lord, for the Personality that you formed in me. I thank you for how my Interests work together and make me unique. I thank you that it's ok to use my Strengths and that you delight in me being the person you created.*
>
> *Lord, I thank you for my unique set of Interests and Needs, for my natural and unnatural Strengths that you use in me. I thank you that you show me how to relax back towards my natural Strengths and that this is good for me. Thank you Lord, that you made each person unique, in order that we can work together to meet each other's Needs, to your Glory.*

Asking for God's direction

We all want to be doing the right thing, but do we look for our inspiration from other people, from the media or from God. Even looking to scripture can mislead us if we think we should be like our favourite character in scripture. God makes us unique and our journey is our story, our purpose is the one uniquely carved out by God for us.

In considering my purpose in life, I am now conscious of how my perceptual filters shape my unconscious thinking. Am I being too direct? Am I over thinking the problem? Should I take this role? How should I approach this family crisis? I now stop myself and ask if what I am thinking is because of my perception? One good friend has often stopped me in conversation to tell me "You're just being Birkman Blue Colin". Now I try to keep at the front of my mind, how other people, who are from different areas of the map, may be seeing an issue differently from me. I no longer assume that my way of doing things is the best way or God's way; rather I turn to God and ask him to show me His way and the best person to address the issue in front of me.

"Ask and it will be given to you"

Matthew. 7 v7.

Asking God to speak into your Strengths, Interests and the roles that you should take on or lay down, is asking for something God wants to speak with you about, because He wants you to be the person He made you to be.

My prayer,

Lord, please keep this learning at the front of my mind so that I do not act without thinking. When I see a need then give me all the Strength to do the best I can in that moment. Then please provide the right person to help with that need into the future. Help me to find the place of contentment, knowing that I am doing all that you ask of me and not doing the things that you ordained for other people.

Lord, where I have learnt to be strong, in ways that do not naturally meet my Needs, show me how to soften my approach to be more like the natural self you intended me to be.

Help me to remember what I Need and speak up so that others will not accidently hurt me. Remembering that their Needs may be hidden, help me to be sensitive to other people's Needs. It is better that I ask, than assume the way that someone wants to be treated.

Knowing your limits

Knowing ourselves not only introduces us to the things we do well and the ways our behaviour supports our Personality, but also shows us how we might behave in ways that do not meet our Needs. Understanding our unnatural Strengths shows us where we need to be kind to ourselves and relax back to our natural selves a little.

For example, while most people at work saw me as structured and ordered, at home my desk is a mess. I once had a housekeeper complain that my carpet was so covered with papers she was not able to vacuum! For many years, I privately assumed that I was simply a hypocrite, but I realise now that my unnatural Strength in being publicly very ordered was not meeting my Need for variety. The chaos on my office floor was an unhelpful attempt at meeting my Need.

Likewise, whilst I can easily give strong leadership or direction, I myself Need a good degree of autonomy. Again, I had assumed I was just a hypocrite, who gave a clear authority to others while not wanting to accept authority from other people, but I now know this was the consequence of a learnt, unnatural Strength. There are still times when being the authority is the right and effective behaviour for me, but I am trying to be kinder to myself and present a less authoritarian perspective to others.

We all want to be successful and I have learnt that, for me, success is more important than having a challenge. However, I now realise that some people thrive on the challenge and I should not stop them, they are simply different from me.

My prayer,

> *Lord, I do not want to be a hypocrite, but I know that there are areas of my Personality Strengths that are different from my Needs. Help me to be the person you made me to be. You are sovereign and you redeem me, you use all of my Strengths. Lord, help me to be obedient to what you ask of me, knowing I can rest and be recharged in the person you made me to be.*

It's Ok to be Human

Self-awareness of our Personality does not remove our unique limitations. We are different from other people and they have different Strengths, just as God intended.

Being forgetful is a limitation most people have, we can't remember everything. If someone forgets my Needs, I should not take that as a personal insult. I can gently and carefully remind them of my Needs and that if they treat me as I Need to be treated, then they will get the best that God intended from me. I also need help to remember other people's Needs so that I can get the best from them.

To be the person God made me to be, means I have to accept that there are many things beyond my design. For example, God did not make me to be a runner. From my earliest days until now, anyone watching me run would know this to be true. It is OK, we can't all be runners. The Sports Teacher, who struck me many times with a plimsoll to try and get me to run faster, did not understand God's design in me. My paperwork has always been a mess and my spelling atrocious; I even used to start board meetings with a one minute opportunity for people to get over my bad spelling on presentations. I am now so grateful for spell checkers! This used to stress me a lot, but now I am simply grateful for other people who have skills I do not have. As a write this, I am conscious that my words are coloured by my Personality and yet I want it to speak to everyone.

The greatest success we can have is through our obedience to God. If He made us with limitations then we have to accept them as part of His intention for us. We can delight in both our Strengths and our limitations, knowing He has put us with other people so that we can be stronger together than apart.

My prayer,

> *Lord, help me to accept, embrace and love the person you made me to be. Help me to be relaxed about the fact that others have different Strengths which I do not have. I want to celebrate the Strengths that you have given others as well as those you have given me. Thank you, Lord, that it is OK to be me.*

Engaging with your Personality

Now, using appendix 2, work through this process yourself so that God can help you to accept and love your Personality. You may find you want to go through the list in order, or you may just want to use it as guidance in your own journey – the choice is yours to make.

Once you have written down as much about your Personality as you can, think about people that you know and consider how different they are from you. Consider how you can adapt your behaviour to better meet their Needs and how you can work together more effectively for God's glory.

It is good to be you. God gave you a unique Personality - do not try to be a different person! Be grateful for the person you are and delight in yourself, as God delights in you.

As Graham Kendrick put it: -

So many times, I have tried to be something that I'm really not
Thinking so much of the things I lack, I forget the things I've got,
Yet it's so hard to take, when the image comes tumbling down,
God gives you grace when you're put in your place, down on your face on the ground.
> *So I'm being myself in Jesus and He's being Himself in me.*
> *I'm being myself in Jesus and that's the way to be.*
> *I'm being myself in Jesus and He's being Himself in me*
> *And the life that He gives is the life that I live and I'm living it naturally.*

Graham Kendrick © 1976 Make Way Music.

Focus on loving your Personality: -

Red corner: -	It is good for me to understand and value the Personality God has given me.
Green corner: -	By valuing and engaging with the range of different Personality elements that God has put into people, I can have better conversations with all sorts of people.
Blue corner: -	By harnessing the full range of different personalities, we can create churches that are more inclusive and build a better future for God's people.
Yellow corner: -	It is part of God's design that we should all work together to respond to His promptings and be obedient to His will, even though some people are very different from me.
Central: -	Christ is the centre of our lives and we see something of His Personality in the wide range of different Personality types. We see this even in some of the more extreme personalities that we might not be comfortable with, yet God would have us love all the different personalities that He has made.

10

Character is made from our beliefs, values and attitudes

For this very reason, make every effort to add to your faith goodness; and to goodness, knowledge; and to knowledge, self-control; and to self-control, perseverance; and to perseverance, godliness; and to godliness, mutual affection; and to mutual affection, love. For if you possess these qualities in increasing measure, they will keep you from being ineffective and unproductive in your knowledge of our Lord Jesus Christ. But whoever does not have them is near-sighted and blind, forgetting that they have been cleansed from their past sins.

2 Peter. 1 v5-9

The premise of this book is that you have a God-given Personality you should love and should not try to change, but alongside this you also have a Character that is learnt. Whilst your Personality is God given and unchangeable, Character can (and should) be changing so as to become more like Christ's.

Personalities that are simply different from each other are neither good nor bad. But we must judge Character, to see if it is good, bad, or a mix of both.

We have explored the first step of understanding and loving the Personality God gave us. Now we need to understand why Character is different from Personality and how we can change our Character.

How behaviour shows Character

We see a person's Character through observing their behaviour, that is, what the person does and says. We say a person is of 'good character' because we see the way they express their beliefs, values and attitudes through their behaviour and agree that what we see is good.

Without seeing a person's behaviour, it is hard to know their Character. We draw assumptions from other people's knowledge about a person through their opinions and who they may associate with. Our beliefs about a person's Character become solid when we directly observe their behaviour and thus make our own judgements about the quality of their Character.

However, it's not always a simple, cut and dried decision when it comes to 'good' Character traits. For example, honesty is considered a good Character trait. However, is being honest always a good Character trait? If you tell me I have food on my chin, then I may be happy with that level of honesty. If you tell me I look really fat, then that may be acceptable if you're my wife, but probably not if you are a stranger in the bus queue. It becomes quite a complex judgement. We decide and then judge if a person is honest or not, according to the degree of dishonesty we may think is acceptable. But that decision is based on our individual beliefs, values and attitudes - everything we know about honesty, we have learnt.

How we learn

From the very first moments after we are born we experience through our senses a broad range of information, ideas and experiences, such as the comfort of a cuddle or the source of food. For each experience we take on board, we decide if it is good or bad, right or wrong. As we grow, the knowledge we are exposed to grows in volume and complexity and we choose to either believe and accept or reject as bad, based on the way we are socialised by the people around us. This constant trade of knowledge and the values we and others put on things, gradually builds our Character.

Our judgement on whether a Character is good or bad has many subtle variations: right or wrong, nice or nasty, harsh or kind etc. We judge each experience with a measure of 'fact or feeling', or a combination of both and it does not always make sense. My seven-year-old granddaughter will only eat green apples; despite me telling her that red apples are just as good, something in her experience has led to the conclusion that she does not like red apples.

Another example: the statement 'I believe Jesus was a carpenter', is for many people, a simple fact of history. While we have no direct evidence (we were not there), the written evidence is enough for most people to assume it is true. It is a statement of fact that has only one key quality - it is either true or false.

The statement, 'I believe Jesus was compassionate' is much more complex. It is either factually correct or not, yet it also has moral qualities which we see as good or bad, which we then attribute to the word compassion. Society generally holds that compassion is a desirable Character attribute, so we would say it is good. However, people attach a wide range of meanings to the word compassionate and can recognise compassion in a very wide range of contexts. It also has complex moral aspects to it, such as: - 'is it good to feel compassion for a criminal?'

Different people will come to different conclusions, so we know that the mix of facts, feelings, tangible and intangible ideas, do not always lead to the same conclusion or judgement.

Learning does not always produce the same outcome in terms of what we choose to believe and how we feel about that belief.

How we form our beliefs

As a child, we trust our parents and the people that our parents trust. Anything that is presented to us through a source that we trust can start to become a fact in our mind. The longer we believe the information we are given, the more it becomes a solid fact. However, many children are presented with information by their parents or other key people, in a way that offers no choice.

It is only as we grow and we reach a point of maturity that we then realise our beliefs are in fact, our choice. We make judgements as to whether the information we receive is true or not. We choose. It is our choice to believe that transforms the information into a fact in our mind. The stronger the evidence appears to us, the more ingrained the fact becomes. As a belief becomes increasingly strong, it can even become an unshakeable belief.

Our choice to keep believing something can be so strong that it can't even be shaken by huge opposing evidence. When a parent is confronted with evidence that their child has committed murder for example, the reaction is typically, "No, I don't believe it". Even when they see the evidence, the confession and the conviction, the parent may continue to disbelieve, seeking reasons not to accept the truth.

This is normal, because the parent has stacked up a whole set of positive beliefs about their child and it is very hard to rationalise evidence that is in conflict with such a strong set of beliefs.

We can group beliefs together around key important people in our lives and these can form a whole set of beliefs, such as with Christianity. The beliefs will be a mixture of facts and feelings that we value and together they may be called 'a belief system', or 'a values system' or even an 'ideology'

The beliefs and values that we have chosen to adopt, then create in us attitudes that are both our sub-conscious and conscious biases, that shape how we behave towards the object of our attitude.

How we measure what is good or bad

When we group together all the things that a person believes, assigns value to and has developed attitudes towards, then we can understand those things as that person's Character. Then we must decide, or judge, whether it is good or not. As children, we may compare another's Character against the Character of a key person like a friend, sibling or parent. As we grow and develop our own Character, then we will tend to judge other people against ourselves.

As we mature, we start to learn that such a small group of comparisons are not enough, so we start to make judgements against a wider or written set of certain standards.

In our western society we have developed etiquette, laws, expectations and opinions by which we can measure Character. In the last few hundred years, printing and other technology have enabled us to communicate and understand these standards more easily. The range and depth of these have grown rapidly and are increasingly driven by media organisations, often with double standards - it is easy to find a newspaper promoting promiscuity as freedom in one section whilst lambasting a politician for promiscuity in another. A wide range of bodies also promote their own standards, be that health, education, food, writers, governments or celebrities.

The standards that society creates change over time. Two hundred years ago it was a commonly held belief that women were second-class humans, with limited education needs, no place in business and no voting rights. The emancipation of women means that most people in western society no longer accept such views today. There are parts of the world however, that still hold such beliefs as being true – people's standards develop at different rates, challenging and re-shaping our beliefs, values and attitudes.

Our culture forms a significant part of who we are and yet our culture is learned. We adopt the culture we live in and it soaks gradually into us as we dwell in it. Our Personality is unaffected by culture. If you take a look at the data in our assessments from anyone in the world, you could not say what culture or country they are from or what sex they are. Personality is God-given and we learn our culture, which is part of our Character.

Culture is in our Character not our Personality

We are both fixed and constantly changing

Personality is fixed and is neither good nor bad. You can say that a certain Personality is more effective or more useful in a certain context, as perhaps with the Firefighter example, but you cannot make a moral judgement about your Personality.

Unlike Personality, your Character is chosen by you and is not fixed. When it comes to Character we very quickly move into much more complex moral issues, which didn't feature in the Personality discussions at all. Character can change slowly as public opinion changes or it can evolve quickly when presented with new evidence, but it is not fixed.

Your beliefs may at times seem unchangeable because of the large stack of evidence you may have accumulated over time and yet even so, they are a choice. Beliefs can be so ingrained that at times people will choose to hold on to them, even to death.

Character is a choice and is malleable. We can change our mind. We make judgements as to whether we think a person's Character is good or bad, by observing their behaviour and comparing it with our preferred standards. For example, being trustworthy is considered by society as a very valuable Character trait. We might judge a person to be trustworthy and therefore see that person's Character as good. Yet this can be easily undermined when that same person is caught lying. We observe the lie and the strength of trust we have is eroded or may even be evaporated completely.

Character is malleable

All salesmen are selfish?

Think back to the example of Gavin Brown the salesman in Chapter 8. For many years, I believed that all salesmen were fundamentally selfish. I now know that some salesmen are selfish and some are not, because I have learnt that selfishness is a Character trait not a Personality type. My belief has changed. I remain cautious because I know from looking at my table of Strengths that my persuasiveness score will probably be much lower than that of a salesman. My 'lack of Strength' in this area might allow a salesman to take advantage of me, which I hate. However, my weakness does not make the salesman selfish.

It may seem difficult to separate in our mind the persuasive Personality from the selfish Character. By understanding that the Personality is God given, I now know that the Personality is not trying to cheat me. I can focus on the person's Character. I can ask myself if there is any evidence that the person is being selfish? Is there any evidence that they are taking an unfair advantage of me? If the answers are no, then my concern may be nothing more than my awareness of the differing personalities between us. If God made the other person to be more persuasive than me, then I should not fear that, rather I should value it.

If, however, there is clear evidence that the person is trying to take advantage of me, that I am being fleeced, duped or taken for a ride, then there is more than a God-given Personality at work. It is a Character that doesn't really care about me, but is trying to cheat me. This is how I know it is an issue with Character.

I do not need to fear my Personality difference, but I do want to defend myself against a selfish Character.

I do not need to fear Personality difference,

I do want to defend against a selfish Character

When we look at a person's behaviour, we can see that it is coloured or shaped by their God-given Personality. We may also see behaviour that is coloured and shaped by their learnt Character. It is important and helpful to know when you are dealing with a Personality difference that is tripping you up, or when it is a Character issue causing a problem. The aim of this book is for people to hang on to their God-given Personality whilst changing their Character so that it increasingly appears like Christ's Character.

When you first start on this journey, you may feel that it's impossible to work out whether behaviour is related to Personality or Character, but over time you'll find that's not true. You can now understand something of your God-given Personality. Therefore, you can ask the question 'Is this my Personality speaking, or is it my Character?' With practise this will become easier and easier and you will be able to answer another important question - is it my Character or theirs?

A further example exploring Personality and Character difference

Remember Yasmin, the new church administrator we met earlier (Page 103) Raymond, one of the Pastors, told Yasmin that Gail would be sharing her office while the building work was undertaken. Raymond offered Yasmin opportunity to talk with him further if she was concerned, but instead she chose to take her concerns to Bruce.

Why did she make that choice? Was it that she feared Raymond? Perhaps she did not trust him? Maybe she thought he would be unsympathetic? Each of these reasons were actually questions in Yasmin's mind about Raymond's Character.

We don't know Raymond that well, but he is a Pastor so it might be reasonable to assume that Yasmin should not be fearful of him. Yasmin has not known Raymond long, but that is not a good reason not to trust him. That leaves the possibility that Raymond may be unsympathetic.

Let's focus on this last option. There are two reasons why Yasmin might think Raymond is unsympathetic: either he *is* unsympathetic, or he *appears* unsympathetic.

We can assume that the role of Pastor was given to him because of his Personality and good Character, so it's not likely that he has learnt to be unsympathetic. It's more likely that Raymond simply appears unsympathetic to Yasmin. We already know that people with a Red Personality are task focused and direct and that Yellow people are indirect in their approach. When an indirect person seeks the opinion of a direct person, it is easy for them to assume that the direct person's speech is unsympathetic, as it is to the point, has no diplomatic padding and can feel blunt. Yasmin may think that Raymond is unsympathetic, but in truth he is just being himself.

There is nothing wrong with Raymond's Character. He is kind and sympathetic, but people can only know this when they get to know his Character. We can easily confuse a Personality trait, which is neither good nor bad, with a Character trait, which can be good or bad.

However, let's assume for a moment that Raymond is rather selfish and therefore did not care about Yasmin's office. His Personality would still be the same, but Yasmin would have been right to pick up signals that Raymond just did not care. It is not possible to hide a selfish Character for long - given a little time, it becomes increasingly obvious why a person is behaving the way they are. At first you might give someone the 'benefit of the doubt' and overlook some apparently selfish behaviour, but eventually the selfish Character will show itself to be what it is.

When you do not know a person's Personality or their Character, it can be very hard to tell what is going on, and easy to make the same mistake as Yasmin by assuming someone's behaviour is a result of Character rather than Personality.

It is only through understanding, that you can establish if the behaviour you're seeing is driven by their Personality, or by their Character.

Your own Personality and Character

Let's imagine for a minute that you are sufficiently concerned about an issue that you need to have a conversation with someone else about it.

Perhaps you are more of an extrovert like Raymond or Gail and find conversation easy. Or you may be more of an introvert, like Bruce or Yasmin and therefore find conversation more difficult.

If you are anxious about the conversation that you need to have, then examine why you are feeling anxious. Is the root of your anxiety simply that your Personality isn't very good at communicating, or is the root in a fear?

If it is a fear that is driving you, then your behaviour is being shaped by the beliefs that you have chosen in your Character. Once you know that it's the belief in your Character is generating the fear, you can begin to change your mind. It may not be easy but it is possible, especially with the help of the Holy Spirit, who will renew your mind.

Focus on Character: -

Red corner: -	God gave me my Personality but I choose my Character.
Green corner: -	When talking with other people, I can appeal to elements of their fixed Personality as well as to the desirable parts of their flexible Character.
Blue corner: -	If I think about it, I can distinguish between benign behaviour originating in Personality and good or bad behaviour originating in Character.
Yellow corner: -	When looking to adopt a set of Characteristics, I choose what to adopt. I cannot choose to have a different Personality but I can choose how to behave.
Central: -	If I see strong elements in a Personality that makes me uncomfortable, I can choose to recognise that God loves variety and that He has made some personalities more extreme than others.

11

Stress behaviours and their temptations

'No temptation has overtaken you except what is common to mankind. And God is faithful; he will not let you be tempted beyond what you can bear. But when you are tempted, he will also provide a way out so that you can endure it.'

1 Corinthians. 10 v13

Humans cannot in reality, be split into the human body, Personality and Character. While considering them separately is helpful, we have to understand that there are complex interactions between these areas.

I have said a number of times that each Personality is neither good nor bad but consists of a unique mix of different traits. You will remember we explored Needs with a number of short stories. We saw that occasionally, when a person does not have their Needs met over a period of time, then there is a risk that they can start to behave in counterproductive ways. The behaviour is attempting to get the persons Needs met, but it is tainted and feels wrong to other people and is counterproductive in nature.

Stress behaviour is unhelpful and sin can amplify this unhelpfulness into genuine negative behaviour. In effect, sin can tempt stress-behaviour into forming a genuine negative Character. Having explored your Personality and now touched on how Character is formed, we need to explore the impact of sin. This chapter will look at how sin relates to the stress behaviour of Personality and then we will look at the more direct impact of sin on our Character.

Example of 'Self-consciousness' Need, stress behaviour

Remember when we talked earlier about the Pastors, Raymond and Bruce, who decided to look at sharing vision for the future of their church? Raymond Needed Bruce to just get to the point, because he has a Red Personality and simply does not Need sensitivity in one to one discussions. However, the Blue Bruce really does Need a diplomatic approach.

You may have spotted their counterproductive behaviours in that story, although it is not easy to 'hear' the tone of voice when a story is written, or to observe the body language through text. Much of stress-behaviour is seen and heard in the body language and tone of voice, which is how we so easily spot that it is unhelpful.

As Bruce explains his desire for a single united vision, you will see that Bruce's statements unhelpfully become more 'wordy' as the discussion progresses. At the same time, Raymond's statements get shorter and more direct until, he says (with a considerable amount of irritation in his voice), "Just tell me what you want me to do!"

Raymond is trying to get Bruce to reduce what he is saying to a focused and direct point, because that is what he Needs. However, Bruce hears Raymond's irritation and sees the unhappy body language, so tries even harder by being more sensitive and diplomatic, which for Raymond, makes the problem even worse.

There comes a point where the tone that Raymond uses becomes hard, clipped or even aggressive and certainly frustrated. As it tips into an unhelpful or counterproductive style, we see stress behaviour taking over. It is not driven by Character or anything else, it is simply Raymond's Personality trying to get its Needs met. However, it can lead to frustration and argument, which in themselves can erode trust and the quality of a relationship.

Christ does not want us to fall out with each-other, rather He wants us to love, honour and value each other. In order to be good brothers, they, like us, have to learn how to avoid this counterproductive behaviour trap.

Sin tempts stress-behaviour

Raymond's directness, when his Need is not met, can be tempted into bluntness or even being plain rude. This can tempt negative Character traits, such as lack of self-control, frustration or anger to reveal themselves.

Likewise, Bruce's indirectness, when his Need is not being met, means he can feel hurt and over sensitive and perhaps find himself withdrawing completely. This can tempt negative Character traits such as selfishness or withdrawing to the point of no longer caring.

When you understand where you might be at risk of tripping into stress-behaviour, you can consciously guard yourself to stop this happening.

For example, If Bruce knows that Raymond is Red, meaning that he is direct and to the point and he can assume his Needs are Red as well, then Bruce can guard himself by thinking before an important conversation about what he wants to say to Raymond. Then Bruce can reduce it to the key issues and present it as succinctly and as focused as possible to best meet Raymond's Needs.

Likewise, if Raymond knows that Bruce has Blue Needs, he can temper his thoughts before he gets into an important conversation, so that when he speaks with Bruce his words are softened and less blunt. That way they do not feel so direct and it reduces the risk of Bruce feeling hurt by what Raymond says.

If both people take account of their differences and make adjustments, they can have successful discussions without falling into the stress-behaviour trap.

A clash of Personality or Character?

I have seen many people fall out with each other, describing their problem as a 'Personality clash'. There was a time when I also accepted this as the reality of life, although I was never comfortable with it. Now I know the truth is, that if two people fail to understand each other and cannot find the language to explain their differences, then it is easy to simply blame their different personalities. I am now certain that blaming a Personality for a clash is just an easy way out of the situation, caused by people being unable or unwilling to understand and accommodate the differences between them. As Carl Jung said in 1958, "Thinking is difficult. Therefore, let the herd pronounce judgement" which is better understood as, "people find thinking difficult, so they are quick to judge, which is much easier".

Personality clash is simply a failure to understand

God-given Personality

Character clash is where we have fundamentally

different values

This is not the same as falling out over Character issues. If I believe that honesty and integrity are essential Character attributes in a person and I find that you don't hold those views, then our relationship will clash and will not work out at a moral level. That is a Character clash, not a Personality clash. I can accept your God-given Personality is different from mine, but I cannot accept a Character whose values are opposed to mine.

Learning a Negative Character trait

There is an old joke about two men in the jungle, that when they hear a tiger running towards them, one man bends down to put his running shoes on. When the other man says, "They won't help you outrun a tiger", the first man replies, "I don't have to outrun the tiger; I just have to outrun you!"

There is a natural desire in our human nature to survive; it is an incredibly strong motivation. I started my career as a Nurse and have cared for many elderly and dying people and I have always been surprised how some people at the end of their life, just do not want to let go. Survival is a very strong motivation.

In order to survive we must breathe, drink, eat and stay warm. As we grow, we learn that we do not have to achieve these basic Needs directly, such as by growing food ourselves. Instead, we exchange skills for money and money for food. At some point in this learning, we can lose sight of simply meeting our needs and start to gather more than we need. It is what we see other people do.

This habit of exceeding our own needs is rewarded by our brain's chemical 'feel good' reaction to gaining new things, which, albeit a brief reward, still encourages the development of a selfish Character. We are encouraged to exceed our needs even further through a barrage of marketing and media that encourages the acquisition of things. We witness this behaviour from an early age as parents respond to their children with things as proxies for love. All this can lead to considering ourselves more important than other people and consequently, a selfish Character can start to form.

We can learn the Character trait of being selfish by distorting our natural motivation of survival into an unnatural belief where we put ourselves first in contexts that go way beyond the need for survival. This can happen with all the aspects of Personality and behaviour we've already talked about, without us even realising.

Stress behaviour tempts negative Character traits

Does our Personality contribute to this? God does not give us selfish personalities. However, we have seen from Raymond and Bruce that Personality differences can lead to unmet Personality Needs, which can produce unhelpful stress-behaviour. Stress behaviour can tempt selfishness to emerge and other stress behaviours can tempt different negative Character traits.

With the story of Raymond and Bruce, it is not difficult to imagine that if Raymond had learned to have an angry Character trait as he grew up, then it might be a short journey to move from his bluntness with Bruce into full blown anger.

Likewise, if Bruce had learned to have a passive-aggressive Character, then it may be a short journey from his verbose stress behaviour into veiled cutting and hurtful language.

While anyone can learn to be aggressive or passive-aggressive, the temptations of stress behaviour may make it easier for a Red person like Raymond to learn to be aggressive and a Blue person like Bruce to learn to be passive-aggressive. This is by no means certain, as it is quite possible for people to learn either, but the temptation of stress behaviour makes certain negative Character traits more likely.

When you consider your Needs, it is possible to imagine the behaviour that might occur if that Need is not met; that is stress behaviour, a counterproductive attempt to meet your own Needs. So a person that Needs time to think things through but doesn't get that time might experience the stress behaviour of procrastination, falling into a place where they become indecisive. If repeated then this can tempt the development of a Character that is indecisive as a habit.

If you have the opposite Need, that is to be decisive, but are constantly faced with ambiguity or lack of freedom to simply get on with it, then you may see your stress-behaviour produce some impulsive and thoughtless action on your part. This can tempt the development of a Character that is bullish and forceful.

Like Bruce and Raymond above, Yasmin and Gail try to meet their own Needs, which can lead to developing negative Character traits. People with Green Needs are at risk of stress-behaviour that can develop into insincerity, selfishness, rebelliousness and impetuousness; those with Yellow Needs are more likely to run the risk of becoming stubborn, arrogant, passive aggressive and selfish.

Selfishness appears with each colour group, which is not surprising as these problems stem from trying to get our needs met. There is nothing wrong with this - it is part of loving ourselves. This love for self only becomes a problem when we make a habit of seeking *more* than we need, putting ourselves first without thinking of other's needs.

Learning negative Character traits

While all Character traits are learnt, both positive and negative, you can see from the above descriptions how Personality Needs can lead to unhelpful stress-behaviour, which can then tempt negative Character traits to develop more easily.

If you develop natural Strengths, that is, ones that meet your Needs, then stress behaviour is much less likely and the temptation of learning negative behaviour will be reduced.

If your Strengths do not meet your Needs, then you are more likely to experience stress-behaviour and be faced with the temptations that such negative behaviour can bring.

Look back at the Strengths pages (Page 124) earlier and see if you identified any unnatural Strengths. Think about the stress-behaviour that you may have experienced and consider whether that has promoted negative Character traits in you. If so, make a note so that you can pray and ask for help to take actions to address those counter-productive Character traits.

Focus on stress-behaviour: -

Red corner: - Stress behaviours can encourage certain negative Character traits to develop.

Green corner: - When I identify my negative Character traits, then I can do something about them; they can be changed because they are my choice. I can choose to minimise the risk of stress-behaviour and ask for help when it appears.

Blue corner: - If I can reduce my stress behaviour and unlearn the negative Character habits, replacing them with Christ's Character, then I will have a much healthier and more positive future.

Yellow corner: - There is a clear logical relationship between stress-behaviour and some negative Character traits, so avoiding stress-behaviour can minimise such Character temptations.

Central: - Even if I have not experienced stress-behaviour in myself, I can recognise it in other people and work with them to meet their Needs and reduce such stress-behaviour, which in turn helps reduce negative Character development.

12

The impact of sin on our behaviour

*This righteousness is given through faith in Jesus Christ to all who believe.
There is no difference between Jew and Gentile, for all have sinned and
fall short of the glory of God, and all are justified freely by his grace
through the redemption that came by Christ Jesus.*

Romans. 3 v22-24

As we have seen, God has given each of us a unique unchanging
Personality. We've also discovered that Character is learnt and
continues to change as our knowledge and experiences grow over
time. In the last chapter, we touched on how stress-behaviour tries to
meet our Need and how such unhelpful behaviour can be magnified
into becoming much more negative in the face of temptation.

Before looking more closely at Character, it is necessary to see where
sin has its voice in this mix of motivations and drives.

Separation from God

Original sin separated us from God and if we are saved, then by God's
grace this relationship is forever restored. This is the gospel of grace.
However, the impact of sin on the way we think and act continues
beyond our salvation, right up to the point when we will see Christ
face to face.

My first Pastor, Don Smith, said to me when I first became a Christian, 'we are like a tin jelly mould that has been dented by a fall. The impact made a dent, that then misshapes us all of our lives'. Resisting the prompting that comes from this sin in us is a different battle for each Christian, but we can fight that battle knowing that, in the end, we can win more often than we lose.

A reminder of the origins of sin

'You are free to eat from any tree in the garden; but you must not eat from the tree of the knowledge of good and evil, for when you eat from it you will certainly die.'

Genesis. 2 v16-17

God made Adam perfect with a unique Personality. He gave Adam one single commandment and this law came with dire consequences. If you eat fruit from the tree of the knowledge of good and evil, you will die – both a physical death and a separation from God, that is, spiritual death.

Adam named the animals and his Character had developed enough to see that no animal was suitable to be his helper. God recognised this and made Eve from Adam.

Adam and Eve were naked, yet not ashamed. (Genesis 2 v25). God had given them Personality, but as they lived and walked with God, it was their Character that was being formed. They were able to take in information and make decisions, yet there was no shame in Adam's thinking.

Who fooled who?

We can assume that Adam told Eve of the commandment in Genesis 2. v17 because God gave this command to Adam before He created Eve.

When the snake said to Eve, "Did God really say, 'You must not eat from any tree in the garden'?" (Genesis. 3 v1) Eve replied quite clearly that this was forbidden, so she obviously knew the commandment, although she misquotes it adding "you must not touch it" when she speaks with the serpent in (Genesis. 3 v3).

Then the temptation from the snake, in Genesis. 3 v4 comes with two lies: -

- You will not die.
- You will be like God, knowing good and evil.

Eve faced a choice: believe what Adam had told her, or believe what the snake was saying.

Eve could have gone back to Adam, told him what the snake had said and asked Adam's opinion. She could have asked the snake why he was contradicting God. She could have asked God why the snake was contradicting Him. However, she made the choice to go and look. She looked at the tree and concluded in verse 6 that 'it looked good to eat and, according to the snake, was also desirable for gaining wisdom'.

Eve chose to eat and be like God!

Eve's downfall

Eve's sin was that she believed that she could rebel, disobey and choose to be like God. She declared that she was independent from God; that God was wrong and she was right.

At best, Eve was calling Adam a liar in not believing what Adam had told her. And at worst, she was calling God a liar. Adam then also clearly called God a liar by eating of the fruit. This is more than breaking God's rule, it is a Character that says, "I know best", I know better than God, I choose to go my own way. This presumption is arrogant selfishness and self-centredness and this is the nature of sin.

Of course, Satan played a part and was also punished by God. But the snake did not force Eve to make the decision that she did, any more than Eve force fed the fruit to Adam. Adam was there, he did not speak up to defend God's instruction, he watched Eve eat, then ate himself, choosing to rebel and disbelieve God.

Adam's shame

The first thing Adam did was to hide in his fear. Before his sin, Adam did not know good and evil, everything was good with just the one commandment. But Adam had eaten the fruit, and now he knew he was wrong, he was ashamed, which is often an outward sign of inward guilt. Dishonesty was just around the corner, because Adam then compounded his sin by blaming God for giving him the woman. (Genesis. 3 v12).

Adam had moved from Satan's temptation of doubt, through a decision that God was not speaking the truth, into his new reality of sin, which brought guilt, fear, shame, death and separation from God.

Pain for now, hope for the future

The first and biggest consequence of sin, was our separation from our Holy God. Adam knew how painful this was, but it is much harder for us to appreciate this. This loss of relationship could not be restored until Christ paid the penalty for our sin on the cross. It is through the cross that we also see the outpouring of God's grace, His love and His forgiveness that can restore our relationship when we choose Him.

The second consequence means that now, we all know the difference between good and evil. We know that the choice between good and bad exists and we have to choose what to believe. However, it is not a simple or balanced choice; the unchecked influence of sin in us, means we are strongly biased towards rebellion against God and the making of selfish choices.

God made Adam with the freedom to choose, but in love protected Adam by the command, "do not eat of the tree of knowledge of good and evil". Did God know that Adam would choose to rebel? Yes (He is an all knowing sovereign)! God knew that two inseparable things would happen: Adam would sin and all of us would inherit that sinful nature and yet we could all be redeemed through Jesus on the cross, restoring that relationship with Himself.

I believe that God knew it was worth the pain of sin and separation, in order that through redemption He could have a relationship with us. He did this because He loves His creation, who through Jesus on the cross, are now free to love Him back.

Between Christ's resurrection and His return

We live in a period where God has forgiven our sin, but as individuals we are still shaped by the effect of sin in us.

As we become more aware of our healthy bodily desires, our God-given Personality Needs and Interests and our learnt Character, we can identify where our thoughts originate and where they are influenced by the effect of sin in us.

If our bodily desires are healthy and our Personality is God given, then the only place left to tackle sin must be within our learnt Character.

This is why we need Christ's Character to dwell in us, to mitigate the influence of sin in our Character choices. He does this through the renewing of our mind by the Holy Spirit, so that our Character is matured from one degree of glory to the next. We must be aware of ourselves and allow the Spirit to do His work. Let me give you a very simple example.

Because our body needs food to function, we are prompted to eat by our hunger. This is not sinful, it's how we were designed, so the battle with sin is not in our bodily desire to eat. Our Personality may shape how we eat - one person may simply see food as fuel, whereas another sees food as an artistic opportunity to stimulate the appetite. One may be happy to eat alone while another sees it as a chance to socialise with others around the table. One may have a regular weekly menu, while another will seek out every opportunity for a new food experience.

While these God-given different Personalities shape our response to hunger in different ways, these responses are not sinful, so the battle with sin is not in our Personality.

When our response to hunger is shaped by our beliefs, values and attitudes, that is, our Character, we then discover the influence of these traits - selfishness, greed, lack of self-control, gluttony or perhaps generosity, compassion and self-control. The problems we have with eating are not in our body or in Personality, but in our Character.

This then is the battleground. Sin tempts us towards the negative Characteristics, but Christ leads us to the positive Characteristics. Our battle with sin is in our choices: without Christ, the sin bias in us will lead us to choose evil; with Christ's Spirit within us to help us, we can choose what is right and good.

This is why we need the power of the Holy Spirit, God's word and the support of others in the Church to help us on the journey of discipleship: so that our Character is increasingly shaped to be like Christ's.

> *'And we all, who with unveiled faces contemplate the Lord's glory, are being transformed into his image with ever-increasing glory, which comes from the Lord, who is the Spirit.'*

2 Corinthians. 3 v18

Sin is rooted in the eating of the tree of knowledge of good and evil

Knowledge shapes our beliefs, values and attitudes - our Character

Sin is rooted in our Character

Focus on sin in us: -

Red corner: -	Sin in us prompts selfish choices. Christ by His Spirit, can and will help us to overcome sinful choices.
Green corner: -	Sin tempts us to cheat to gain advantage, to be selfish; but costs us in relationship every time. Christ's Character enables us all to be winners.
Blue corner: -	Stress behaviour combined with sin's temptations always lead to a worse future, Christ's Character in us leads to a better future for us all.
Yellow corner: -	Separation from God was dealt with by Jesus on the cross. To overcome sin requires a daily routine of allowing Christ's Character to flourish and dwell in us by His Spirit.
Central: -	Christ's Character in us gradually puts our Character back to a balanced position, no longer being distorted by sin.

13

The fruit of the Spirit and the Character of Christ

'But the fruit of the Spirit is love, joy, peace, forbearance, kindness, goodness, faithfulness, gentleness and self-control. Against such things there is no law.'

Galatians. 5 v22-23

Before we consider the Character of Christ, it is worth spending a moment on His humanity and Personality.

Jesus was wholly human, born of woman, with all the natural strengths and desires of any other person. He cried when He was hurt and He grew hungry and thirsty like all other people. He was conceived by God, not man, which meant that he did not inherit from Adam the desire to sin that came from eating from the tree of knowledge of good and evil.

If you look to the Bible to understand Jesus' Personality, then you will have a difficult task, because His mission was to address sin, the route of our Character problems. There are plenty of scriptures that describe Jesus' perfect Character and yet very few that reflect His Personality. I can argue from scripture that when you look at the map, Jesus clearly showed Personality from each of the four colours: -

His Green Personality

Jesus showed His Green Personality in His remarkable ability to communicate, either directly as in the 'Sermon on the Mount', or less directly through parables.

His Blue Personality

We see Jesus' Blue creativity in John 1 where Jesus is described as the Word, through whom all things are created.

His Yellow Personality

Jesus showed His Yellow nature through His grasp of the Old Testament scripture and how He understood the order of these things, especially the process by which salvation would come to man through His own actions ordained by God the Father.

His Red Personality

We also see Jesus' Red action orientation, such as when He overturned the temple tables or turned water in to wine.

What was Jesus' Personality?

While we can see from scripture certain events that hint at each personality type, we cannot say what Jesus' personality was like, yet we know that He was fully human.

Perhaps the only way that we can come close to understanding Jesus' Personality is by looking at the way the Bible mentions a partner suitable for Jesus. This is illustrated not by a particular individual but by a large and diverse group of people, that is, the Church, or the Bride of Christ (Revelation 21 v2). As Dr Birkman said, "God has sprinkled His personality among us". If we could understand the sum total of all the Church's individuals Personalities, then we might come close to seeing the reflected Personality of God who made us in His image.

That Jesus is both fully human and fully God in one person is a mystery we cannot understand. It is the perfect joining of the divine and the human in one person.

The Character of Jesus

Was Jesus born with a fully formed Character, or did His Character grow as He grew? Again we cannot certainly know, but Luke describes how the young *Jesus grew in wisdom and stature and in favour with God and man'* (Luke. 2 v52). Wisdom is the application of knowledge and experience in a very successful and effective way, which forms part of our beliefs and values. If Jesus grew in wisdom, then He was not born with fully formed beliefs, values and attitudes.

Is it even possible to talk about Jesus having beliefs? Jesus didn't have to believe in Himself, He knew Himself. In fact, later in His life Jesus said that He only did what the Father taught Him (John. 8 v28), meaning that He could not have known everything from His birth.

What we do know, is that whilst Jesus didn't know everything from the start, He believed His Father and trusted in His guidance. Whether or not this illustrates beliefs as we know them, Jesus clearly had a set of beliefs that were so certain that we can describe them as values.

So how can we describe Jesus' values and attitudes, which we see as the Character of Christ? One approach would be to simply read the Bible and identify each Character trait Jesus demonstrates, but this would form a very long list of subtle Characteristics, some of which He clearly positively values and some He strongly rejects.

Instead, let's look at just how much information we can glean about the Character of Christ in just one chapter of Luke: -

Luke 4:2	*He valued strength and resisted the Devils temptations.*
Luke 4:4	*He valued the truth of scripture and used it against Satan.*
Luke 4:8	*He valued worshiping the one and only true God.*
Luke 4:12	*He valued the truth and knew there was no need to test God.*
Luke 4:21	*He had confidence in who He was.*
Luke 4:28	*He spoke out the truth even if it made him unpopular.*
Luke 4:38	*He had compassion for the sick and rebuked evil.*
Luke 4:43	*He was determined to undertake His task.*

Perhaps you can read the rest of Luke and list all the Character attributes you find?

Character Traits

Rather than writing a long list, let's focus on Character trait words that summarise a large number of characteristics.

Perhaps the easiest way to describe the Character of Jesus, is to explore Paul's description to the Galatians of the 'fruit of the Spirit' which are all Character traits.

Love

Love is the first - and greatest - Character trait and summarises all that is good. It forms the basis of all we know about God and His Character, everything else is hollow and empty without love.

> *"Love the Lord your God with all your heart and with all your soul and with all your mind'. This is the first and greatest commandment. And the second is like it: 'Love your neighbour as yourself.' All the Law and the Prophets hang on these two commandments."*
>
> Matthew. 22 v37-40

Simply put: love God, love yourself and love your neighbour.

The Bible gives us a great definition of love: *"This is how we know what love is: Jesus Christ laid down his life for us. And we ought to lay down our lives for our brothers and sisters."* (1 John. 3:16). Only a chapter later Paul says,

"This is how God showed His love among us: He sent His one and only Son into the world that we might live through Him." (1 John. 4:9).

There is nothing weak about this kind of love.

God's desire to have a relationship with His people, to love His people, was so strong that He sent His one and only Son to die on the cross in our place. Jesus' desire to have a relationship with His people, to love His people, was so strong that He laid down His own life for us.

Paul's understanding of love is that our relationships are so important that we should be prepared to lay down our life, desires and wants, in order to give preference to our brothers and sisters.

This is love; it is much stronger than a feeling of affection or a warm attachment. Some people feel that the reference to laying down your life, is only about literal death, giving your actual life for the sake of someone else. While this is ultimately true, it is a rarity.

The daily reality is that a husband lays down his desires in order to prefer his wife, to bless her and meet her needs. A wife does the same for her husband. It is also true that if we listen to God's prompting we may find, at any moment, God may ask us to lay down what we are doing in order to be a blessing to someone else.

What might this look like in everyday life? It may mean a Yellow person laying down their preference for making lists in order for a Blue colleague to think about possibilities and ideas. A Green person, who is energised by the new and novel, may lay down that desire so as to visit a museum with a Yellow person, who loves to spend time exploring history. A Blue person might take off their headphones in order to take a Red person out into the country in order to delight in the great outdoors. A Red person may stay quiet and not offer a solution to fix it, so a Blue person can explain how they are feeling, to simply 'get it off their chest'.

Love requires a sacrifice of our own preference in order to bless the other person.

Love is a Character issue. It is a decision we make based on our beliefs and our values that produces in us a range of attitudes and subsequent actions, that together we call love. It can be eroded when confronted with behaviour such as lies, disloyalty, cruelty, unkindness or even hate, because such behaviour undermines love.

Love without actions is a sterile set of beliefs that are untried and may be nothing more than feelings. Only when we commit to act do we learn both the cost of love and the joy of being loved.

Joy

Joy takes many forms. Sometimes we see it when we tickle a child and see the pleasure and happiness it causes. A pantomime can evoke much laughter; but Paul is referring to joy that is more than physical.

Another form of Joy comes from the Personality. If you have a Blue high musical Interest, then listening to a well-performed piece of music can produce great pleasure and happiness. Red people might find great joy in being outdoors. Winning a competition or argument can be a real delight to Green people, whereas Yellow people are more likely to find joy in working through a puzzle to a successful conclusion.

Joy comes when we achieve and succeed and yet Paul is referring to more than satisfaction. What he is really referring to is a spiritual joy.

Joy is also a Character trait. When we make good choices and delight others, we also enjoy the great pleasures of our good choices, especially when we make others happy. Of course our greatest joy can be found as we dwell on what God has done for us through Jesus' sacrifice as Paul said,

> *"And I pray that you, being rooted and established in love, may have power, together with all the Lord's holy people, to grasp how wide and long and high and deep is the love of Christ".*

Ephesians. 3 v18

Therefore, if we are to see the joyful fruit of the Spirit, then we need Christ's Character to help us ensure that we continually make choices that bring pleasure and happiness to God, to other people and ourselves.

Peace

Peace is important to the body. Finding a bee caught up in your clothing may lead to instant panic with the body reacting with a clear 'fight or flight' mechanism, which pumps adrenalin around the body before you have even consciously recognised the fear. Peace is more than just the body being free from fear.

Peace is something that might be found through meeting our Personality Needs. A Blue person may find peace in certain music or time alone, whereas a Green person is more likely to find peace in knowing that they have been heard. A Red person may find peace at the end of a long run outdoors and a Yellow person may find peace in knowing the plan has worked out as expected. For some peace is on a silent and remote hill, for others it may be fully engrossed in their reading in the middle of a chaotic café, we are each so different. Peace is also more complex than meeting our Personality Needs and making space to engage with our Interests.

Peace as a fruit of the Spirit has a great depth of meaning - peace with God and the peace of God are very different. We have peace with God, through accepting the grace of God's salvation through Jesus' sacrifice on the cross; this restores our relationship with God that Adam lost. We are no longer at war, we have peace with God. Similarly, when we accept the person we are, we can be at peace with ourselves and then cease striving to be someone else.

The 'peace of God' is more to do with our faith. We follow Christ and in doing so we believe things which are unseen.

Our faith is found in what we hope for in Christ, the assurance of our salvation and the hope for our future. Such peace is a choice and is subject to our beliefs; it is therefore clearly a Character trait. The level of our confidence in our belief is our faith and God gives faith, it is a fruit of the Spirit.

The greater our belief, the greater is our faith and the greater is the peace of God in us.

Faith is an issue of trust as Jesus said,

> *"Look at the birds of the air; they do not sow or reap or store away in barns, and yet your heavenly Father feeds them. Are you not much more valuable than they?"*

Matthew. 6 v26

The more confident our faith is in Jesus and His promises, the more we trust, then the greater is our peace. Faith is our choice, but also God gives faith through His Spirit. This is seen in the importance of the story of the man whose son was ill in Matthew. 9 v24, where the man says "I do believe; help me overcome my unbelief!"

Patience

Patience is the ability to show restraint and tolerance with others, even when provoked, not with a heart of frustration, rather with a heart of peace and love. Patience is also strong and is not selfish; it does not rush to conclusions and is slow to anger.

This Character trait is demonstrated by Jesus throughout His life on earth and most importantly in the time from the Garden of Gethsemane through to His crucifixion. Jesus remained patient and determined, never turning away from the journey to the Cross. In the Garden, the disciples could not even stay awake with Him and while at first He criticised them for sleeping, He let them sleep. (Matthew. 26 v36-46).

Jesus continued to show tolerance throughout the many provocations on the journey to the cross, with the most extreme provocation on the cross itself. Yet He showed restraint and tolerance, even when the Father turned His back on Him.

Patience may be a physical requirement when hunting or fishing, but Christ' spiritual patience is much greater than that.

Patience can be found in the introverted Blue and Yellows as they take time to think through a problem or carefully restore an antiquity to perfect condition. Extroverted Red and Green people on the other hand, may not see the need for patience as they fix a leak or win a football match. However, Paul was writing about a spiritual patience that goes beyond our physical and Personality natures.

Spiritual patience is the peaceful and loving restraint and tolerance, in the face of unreasonable provocation and frustration. It requires a strength that may be beyond our Personality's ability, which is why it is a Character choice and therefore a fruit of the Spirit.

This Character trait is essential for successful relationships. It tempers the body's 'fight and flight' response so that we are slow to anger and can be both patient and persistent, but that does not mean capitulation, as it comes with determination and endurance.

Kindness

Most people, when asked, will know what they mean by kindness. It is being friendly, generous and considerate but also includes subtleties such as tenderness, concern and thoughtfulness, showing that you care about people.

Green and Blue folk are more focused on people than they are on the tasks that are required. This might give the impression that they are kind, but their sociability with others may be more about their own Needs than about being kind to others. Red and Yellow people are more likely to focus on the task first, which might give an impression that kindness is less important, but a task focus might be in order to help a person. So Personality does not give much of a clue in to the kindness that Paul refers to.

Kindness is a choice, and since our beliefs inform our motivation as to how to choose, it is part of our Character. Christ's motivation is love. He values each of us highly and He is also kind to us. We see this in Luke. 6 v32-36 when Jesus describes the motivation behind actions. Jesus shows that being kind to people who are kind to us has no great value - even sinners love those that love them. God showed kindness to the ungrateful and wicked. This is the type of kindness that we want to nurture in our Character, the kindness that we see in the 'Good Samaritan' or the father of the 'Prodigal Son'.

Kindness to the wicked means choosing to be kind in the way that Christ chose to die for us on the cross. This is the kindness that Paul is writing about.

Goodness

Goodness isn't about whether we are 'good' or 'bad' at doing something. Whilst we might be 'good at something', this is not the same as being morally good, or demonstrating goodness. Our personalities seek out things that we are passionate about or Need. Whether extrovert or introvert, people or task focused, we all have different passions, but they are not good or bad in themselves.

It would seem that demonstrating goodness in our behaviour, is something we have to learn. As we grow we learn that being good is important. The number of times I have told my growing children to be good when visiting Grandma is beyond counting!

We see that even without Christ, some people learn to be good; as their knowledge grows and they adopt good values, we can see that a moral Character trait of goodness appears. However, selfishness is never far from us and we see many good people exposed as having hidden poor morals, people who help some while quietly abusing others. Demonstrating a Character of moral goodness is relatively easy compared to being morally good to the core. In truth, we only find such pure goodness in Christ.

Jesus described Himself as the 'Good shepherd' in John. 10 and His message of the Gospel means 'Good News'. Most importantly, it is His sacrifice in laying down His life for us that really demonstrates His goodness.

So, goodness is seen most clearly as the sum of Character traits that we know is good for our society. Being good is not about behaving as a 'good boy or girl' but summarises the set of moral behaviours that when seen by others, are described as being good.

Faithfulness

While key Character behaviours such as honesty and integrity relate to faithfulness, the loyalty and devotion to following God's ways are central to our meaning here. Such devotion requires us to be 'full of faith' as well as loyal.

Our Personality can appear faithful to people or to a task. A Yellow person's attention to detail can be interpreted as a faithful application to a task. A Red person may work faithfully at fixing something that is broken. Similarly, a Blue great artist may make a faithful interpretation of someone in a portrait. A Green person's passion for variety, can also be interpreted as being less faithful to the task. However, none of these really relate to the fidelity of friends, devotion to God or obedience to God's will, which are the heart of what Paul wrote about this fruit.

Our ability to be truly faithful to people and God is a Character trait we learn and develop. It requires us to trust and to be confident in that trust. We see Jesus' faithfulness demonstrated on the cross, when He did not waver from the task God had given Him. Because we choose to believe Jesus, we see His faithfulness to us. When we are confident of the truth and we value other people and God, then we choose to be faithful to God and to other people.

Gentleness

Gentleness is not brutish, violent or controlling, rather it is mild and tender. Yet it is not weak or passive. Physical gentleness is a necessity of successful parenthood, especially in the early vulnerable years of life.

The Red person tends to be assertive in the sense of directing and controlling, or being authoritative. However, this does not imply that they are hard or rough. Although the direct and 'to the point' language of the Red person might appear hard and insensitive, it carries no malice.

Likewise, the Blue person who has a more sensitive and diplomatic personality may appear gentler, but underneath have no compassion. Paul was speaking of a gentleness of Character, greater than our physical or Personality trait.

Many people learn how to be polite and diplomatic and their work may require certain gentleness. However, the gentleness we see in Christ is the ability to remain gentle under duress. In the face of the interrogation of Pilate, Herod and the Chief Priests and the accusations of the crowd, Jesus remained peaceful and gentle. As the Son of God, He could call down the angels and the wrath of God at any time, but He remained at peace.

As Jesus said of Himself,

> *"Come to me, all you that are weary and are carrying heavy burdens, and I will give you rest. Take my yoke upon you, and learn from me; for I am gentle and humble in heart, and you will find rest for your souls. For my yoke is easy, and my burden is light".*

> Matthew. 11 v28-30

This is the gentleness we need in our Character and it can only be found in Christ.

Self-control

We can all relate to losing our temper, breaking our diet or giving-in to our selfish desires. It is also possible to be so-stressed or 'uptight' that a person can be too self-controlled like a zealot or extremist. So there is good self-control and an unhealthy self-control.

Physically we should be self-controlled and balanced in everything we do for our body. Some people put great effort into controlling the physical desires in order to keep their body looking good, but this is rarely driven by the body itself and usually relates to self-image and self-esteem or our concerns about how others will view and like us.

Our bodies may find another person very attractive. It is our self-control that stops us reacting to the urges that such attraction produces in us. We hopefully choose to try to direct our physical passion appropriately, although the rate of infidelity and divorce and family breakdown tell us how poor our self-control is.

Paul is really talking about our Character having mastery over our bodies and its drives, our Personality and its Needs, as well as the impact of sin on our behaviour. It is only when we have control over all these aspects of ourselves, that we can say we have complete self-control. The fact is, we all sin and fall short of the glory of God. As a result, we require the forgiveness that Christ earnt for us on the cross.

This shows that we do not have the ability within us to be fully self-controlled. Only with Christ in us, with His prompting and His strength through the Holy Spirit, do we really have hope of self-control.

Self-control is the most important Character trait next to love. While love is like the capital letter that starts the list of the fruit of the spirit, Self-control is the full stop. Together love and self-control bracket all the other fruit and together they sum up the Character of Christ. These are the great moral Character traits of Christianity and of Christ Himself. When we demonstrate such Character traits, other people will know that Christ dwells in us as they see our behaviour overcoming all things by the power of the Holy Spirit within us.

I am not suggesting that it is easy to have self-control over your passions or sin at work in you, but it is the very sharpest point of the battle in our minds. While we are nothing without love, the one fruit of the Spirit that we need above the rest, is self-control.

Focus on the Character of Christ: -

Red corner: -	Christ's Character is summed up as the fruit of the Spirit, which we need.
Green corner: -	In order to have successful relationships we need these positive Character traits in our lives.
Blue corner: -	We will have a happier and more fulfilled future if we can see our lives lead by such Character traits.
Yellow corner: -	Love and self-control are the top two Character traits we need in our lives, they summarise them all.
Central: -	It is loving self-control that enables a balance in all we do and in so doing we avoid extremism.

14

Inviting Christ to be Himself in you

"You did not choose me, but I chose you and appointed you so that you might go and bear fruit—fruit that will last—and so that whatever you ask in my name the Father will give you. This is my command: Love each other."

John. 15 v16-17

Defining our overarching goal in life is not easy. It may be to produce offspring that have a better life than our own, or it may be to make an impact on society that goes beyond our life, but for many, survival is a big enough goal.

A major goal for most of our lives is to see growth in ourselves, to become more than we are and to finish the race well (2 Timothy. 4v7). The most important way a Christian can demonstrate this growth, is by producing the fruit of the Spirit and this is only achieved as Christ makes His home in us and dwells in us through His Spirit.

Growth means change and in this context, to change in order to become like Christ. We must ensure we change the correct things. We should not try and be like someone else. No, we must be ourselves; comfortable and self-aware of the body we have and the Personality God has given us. The change we must work for is to have the Character of Christ in us.

We have each inherited sin, the desire to be independent from God, and it is this self-centredness, this selfishness, that is our daily battle within our mind. This battle is not about the desires of our bodies or our personalities, although both can tempt sin in us and we can use both as excuses for our sinful behaviour. Without God, we are all biased by sin in us and will fail, so our daily battle is in our Character, where we must choose to sin or not to sin.

Fortunately, we have Jesus Christ, who is perfect and who has promised that He would come and live in us so we could have ready access to His Character. We do not need to look up in a book how to behave, but to simply listen to God who is living in us through His Spirit:

> *"Remain in me, as I also remain in you. No branch can bear fruit by itself; it must remain in the vine. Neither can you bear fruit unless you remain in me."*

John. 15 v4

The image of the vine producing fruit is used frequently by Jesus throughout His teachings and again by Paul in his letter to Galatians. The vine itself draws water and food from the soil, to feed the branches that will then blossom and produce fruit. You can take a vine shoot, cut it and then also cut a separate vine stem and then bind them together. The wound will heal and the cutting will now be part of the plant.

This grafting process means that the new vine will be fed and watered by the original vine. Jesus uses this image to describe how we are grafted into God. We are cut off from our old life as we accept Jesus. Jesus was then 'cut' for us on the cross, in order that we could be grafted into Christ, consequently we are able to receive 'Godly sap' through Jesus. By His grace and through His Spirit, He feeds and waters us in order to produce fruit, good fruit, the fruit of the Spirit.

An aside about knowing your ministry

I have been asked many times by other people what I think their ministry is. For me the answer is always the same. When you come across a fruit tree, you don't stick an aspirational label on it, such as 'I hope one day this will be an apple tree'; rather we patiently wait. If the tree is rooted where it can be fed and watered, then in good time it will produce fruit. When you discover the fruit it produces are apples, only then can you say, "Here we have an apple tree."

In the same way, if you want to know what your gifting is for the church; then stay grafted into the vine of God, drawing your spiritual food and water from Him. In time you will produce spiritual fruits and other people will see and say that you are an Apostle, Prophet, Evangelist, Teacher or Pastor (Ephesians. 4 v11). Perhaps you have the gift of prophesying, serving, teaching, encouraging, giving or leading (Romans. 12 v6-8). Or perhaps by God's grace you have wisdom; knowledge, faith, healing, miracles, prophesy, tongues or interpretation of tongues (1 Corinthians. 12 v7-11).

It is only by observing the fruit that shines through our behaviour, that we can then identify what the gifting is.

The Spiritual fruit reveals the Spiritual Gift

I once planted a plum tree in my garden. In the first spring, it produced many flowers, but not a single fruit. I spoke to the tree and encouraged it. In the second, there were many flowers but again not a single fruit. I reminded the tree that God said if you don't produce fruit you will be cut down and thrown in the fire. The following spring it was full of flowers, I even went around with a small brush to ensure the flowers were being pollinated. But for the third season it failed to produce fruit.

So I cut the branches down and used the stump as a base for a bird table. My Pastor, Don, came to visit and we sat in our small garden for tea. He noticed the bird table and I recounted my story, expecting him to be impressed by my youthful spirituality. Don laughed and laughed. He then explained that plum trees never produce fruit in the first three years after planting. One more year and the branches would have been strong enough for the tree to produce fruit.

What a fool I was. Fruit comes in the right season and if I had listened to God, the great gardener, then I would have heard the truth about patience, rather than making a decision in my own strength and the arrogance of my youth.

How can we have the Character of Christ in us?

There are two ways that humans can attempt to have a Character like Christ.

Firstly, you could try to be like a good person.

Many people believe that it is possible to study Christ and his teachings and as they learn about His Character they can then simply adopt His beliefs, values and attitudes and in doing so, they will be like Him. It requires tremendous will-power, dedication, self-discipline and effort. Like a high wire act or trapeze artist, you have to be very fit and well-practiced to avoid falling.

Trying to be a good person is the best ever description of a religious approach to building your Character. The hope is that careful attention to the Law and daily perfect discipline will create behaviour that imitates Christ.

People all over the world try to adopt behaviour of good people. They study the ways of Mahatma Gandhi; Mother Theresa, Mohamed, The Dali Lama, or even Jesus. While this religious approach can produce good people, it ultimately fails because in each case it relies on the person to change using their own strength.

There was a classic TV advertisement in 2002 where an Indian man beats his Hindustan Motors Ambassador car to change its shape. He drives it into a wall, gets an elephant to sit on it, he beats and beats it until it looks like a Peugeot 206, the car of his dreams. However, no matter what it looks like, under the hood it is still the same old engine, chassis, suspension and brakes. The weaknesses of the original car are still there under the surface.

This is what people do when they try to simply imitate the Character of a great example. They change the way they behave so that they look like the person they wish to imitate, but the Character underneath is still the same person, fighting against their own sinful nature, their selfishness, using their own strength.

This is the very same sin that Adam and Eve fell into. They thought that they could choose using their own strength and wisdom, they tried to be independent of God and of course failed. This is sin.

Salvation

> *"I am the way and the truth and the life. No one comes to the Father except through me."*

John.14 v6

The second way to be Christ-like in our Character, is through Salvation, **which is the only way** that successfully and fundamentally changes us. Having acknowledged that we cannot change on our own and that we need Jesus as Lord, we repent of our sin and then invite Him into our lives and ask Him to renew and change our minds.

This is salvation. Jesus then plants a seed within our Character, which Paul refers to as a deposit.

> *'Guard the good deposit that was entrusted to you—guard it with the help of the Holy Spirit who lives in us'.*

2 Timothy. 1 v14

After salvation, put on the full armour of God, as Paul said in his letter to the Ephesians,

> *'Stand therefore, and fasten the belt of truth around your waist, and put on the breastplate of righteousness. As shoes for your feet put on whatever will make you ready to proclaim the gospel of peace. With all of these,*

take the shield of faith, with which you will be able to quench all the flaming arrows of the evil one. Take the helmet of salvation, and the sword of the Spirit, which is the word of God.'

Ephesians. 6 v14-17

Salvation, this is the real Good News, it is the genuine article that brings authentic change. Genuine change on the inside is what is required, as Jesus said,

"Woe to you, scribes and Pharisees, hypocrites! For you are like whitewashed tombs, which on the outside look beautiful, but inside they are full of the bones of the dead and of all kinds of filth."

Matthew. 23 v27

The seed is planted at salvation, but if it is not fed and watered, it fails to grow. We need Christ to help us by His Holy Spirit from within.

Abiding in Christ

"Abide in me as I abide in you. Just as the branch cannot bear fruit by itself unless it abides in the vine, neither can you unless you abide in me. I am the vine, you are the branches....... My Father is glorified by this, that you bear much fruit and become my disciples."

John. 15 v4-8

Once we have been grafted into the vine by salvation, we must remain in the vine and draw the sap from the roots, letting God feed and water us spiritually.

The words 'abiding' or 'dwelling' have become a little lost in our language, partly because 'life' or 'where we live' is thought of in terms of activity or being busy, rather than resting or soaking. So, consider abiding as a long soak in the bath, a slow walk in the country, or sunbathing on the beach.

To abide in Christ means 'to stay close to Him', in fact so close to God that we can become part of Him. We do this through prayer; by asking the Holy Spirit to speak, then listening and responding. As Mike Pilavachi, of the 'Soul Survivor' Watford church said, "We need to dial down (our effort) to hear Him". This reflects the way that Elijah on Mount Horeb, did not hear God in the wind, or the earthquake or the fire, but in the gentle whisper (1 Kings. 19 v12).

As we abide in God, prayer becomes natural and part of each decision and everyday life. The Evangelist Smith Wigglesworth apparently said, "I don't ever pray any longer than twenty minutes….. but I never go twenty minutes without praying."

The starting place of prayer, as the Psalmist said, is "Enter his gates with thanksgiving and his courts with praise; give thanks to him and praise his name" (Psalm. 100 v 4). Dwelling for a moment on what we should praise and thank God for helps us get the context of our prayers right. Reading the Bible, our final authority, adds to our understanding and gives opportunity for the Holy Spirit to speak into each situation. The more we do this, the more His words will come easily to us in each moment that our Character has to deal with.

Talking with other Christians about the truth of Jesus is another way to gain a wider perspective of who God is and what He has done. Reading good authors can broaden our perspective about God, but we always need to check that what is said does not disagree with the Bible.

God gives us things to do, but if we then continue with something beyond what God has asked of us, we can then make those same things into a distraction from God Himself.

We need to consciously review where we are investing our time and compare it to what God has asked of us. Some things are legitimate but not personally helpful, as Paul wrote about in his first letter to the Corinthians:

> "I have the right to do anything," you say—but not everything is beneficial.
>
> "I have the right to do anything"—but not everything is constructive.
>
> 1Corinthians. 10 v23

When a vine is grafted into another vine, it actually has very little to do. The rising sap forces new growth, which produces flowers and then fruit. This is what Jesus said we should do, abide and wait on Him.

Becoming conscious of Personality and Character

In life, at every choice we have to make, at every decision and whenever we have to take action, there are four steps we can take, or questions we can ask. These are based on our understanding that we have a body, a God-given Personality, a Character we want to change to be like Christ and an ongoing battle with sin.

Body

> *Do you not know that your bodies are temples of the Holy Spirit, who is in you, whom you have received from God? You are not your own; you were bought at a price. Therefore, honour God with your bodies.*

> 1 Corinthians. 6 v19-20

Our physical bodies have needs, which is how they are designed. Once we recognise those needs for what they are, we can ensure that our Character can choose to meet them appropriately.

If you want to change your body, then eat well, exercise well and sleep well. Do not assault your body with substance abuse or other things that are bad for it. Your body is where you live - look after it! Making these good decisions comes from having a Christ-like Character that obeys the command to look after our bodies.

The first question to ask yourself, is whether the issue before you is simply your physical body presenting a desire? If yes, what is the appropriate response? Or is the issue more than your body speaking?

Personality

'For you created my inmost being; you knit me together in my mother's womb. I praise you because I am fearfully and wonderfully made; your works are wonderful, I know that full well'.

Psalm. 139 v13-14

In whichever way God made your unique Personality, accept and delight in the Interests and Needs that God has given you. If you have learnt to be different from how you were designed, then, where you can, relax back to the Personality God gave you.

Of course, we cannot use our Personality as an excuse for our behaviour. We must also adapt our behaviour, so that at times we might lay down our own Needs and Interests, in order to better meet another person's Needs. This is how we love others and love, is the heart of God.

This is being yourself in Jesus; being the person God meant you to be.

The second question then, asks if the matter in hand is being driven by your God-given Personality's Interests or Needs? If yes, what is the appropriate response? Or is the issue more than your body and Personality speaking?

Character

Your Character is shaped and developed by every bit of knowledge and wisdom you have gained through your life. This information forms your beliefs. The beliefs that are important to you then form your values and create your attitudes. It is these beliefs, values and attitudes that shape your decisions and colour your behaviour – this is what other people see as your Character.

It is here that we want to see ourselves change to be like Christ. We recognise that Jesus' Character is perfect and if we have the same Character as Jesus, then our lives and other people's lives will be very much better indeed.

The third question then, is to ask if our behaviour agrees and conforms to our understanding of expectations and truths that we know about Jesus' Character.

If not, then your belief, value or attitude is flawed. Ask The Holy Spirit to renew your mind so that your Character will reflect Christ's Character. Ask Him to be Lord of the moment, Lord of your choice, Lord of your behaviour. It will require strength to do the right thing, but if we ask the Holy Spirit for strength, He will give it.

In the same way, the Spirit helps us in our weakness. We do not know what we ought to pray for, but the Spirit himself intercedes for us through wordless groans.

Romans. 8 v26

This is where we should focus our effort to make changes in who we are, letting Jesus be Himself in us.

Sin

Therefore do not let sin reign in your mortal body so that you obey its evil desires. Do not offer any part of yourself to sin as an instrument of wickedness, but rather offer yourselves to God as those who have been brought from death to life; and offer every part of yourself to him as an instrument of righteousness. For sin shall no longer be your master, because you are not under the Law, but under grace.

Romans. 6 v12-14

A fourth question can follow the three above. Is the issue at hand more than your body and Personality speaking or an incorrect Character at work?

Are you being tempted to act in a way that is rooted in the selfishness of sin in you? If yes, then you know that you need God's help to choose the right behaviour to overcome sin. This is the battle with sin, as Terry Virgo said "it is not like a battle, it **is** a battle".

The battle is not easy

If anyone loves me, he will obey my teaching. My Father will love him, and we will come to him and make our home with him."

John. 14 v23

Of course, making the right choice is hard work. Dallas Willard said in his book 'The Great Omission', "Grace is opposed to earning, not effort".

But as Christ reveals His Character in us and we ask for His help, we learn from Him. As a result, our beliefs, values and attitudes can, over time, change to be like that of Christ.

Our Personality, with His Character

Jesus said in John. 14 v15-31, the Father would send the Holy Spirit to dwell in us, make a home in us and would teach us all things, reminding us of what Jesus has said. Persistently asking for the Holy Spirit's help and checking our decisions with Him takes effort, but with just a little more each day, it is surprising what God can do.

The Holy Spirit then is our daily helper. How we listen to Him varies based on what we have been taught, but at its simplest we ask the Spirit, "what would Jesus do?" Some people even wear a wristband to remind them of this key question.

However, the Spirit does more than simply answer questions, He also renews our mind.

Paul wrote in his letter to the Church in Rome,

> *'Therefore, I urge you, brothers and sisters, in view of God's mercy, to offer your bodies as a living sacrifice, holy and pleasing to God—this is your true and proper worship. Do not conform to the pattern of this world, but be transformed by the renewing of your mind. Then you will be able to test and approve what God's will is—his good, pleasing and perfect will.'*

Romans. 12 v1-2

Note that Paul does not say transform your body. What he does say, is that we shouldn't be conformed to the world. Paul knows that the world is corrupt from Adam's sin, and that the world sets its own standards that are not God's standards.

Rather than being like the world, Paul says, be transformed by the renewing of your mind. To be transformed we must be dealing with our malleable Character, not our God-given Personality.

This is the process of allowing Christ Character to grow in you so that your Character becomes like Christ's.

Christ being Himself in you!

We have summarised the contents of this chapter in Appendix 3 in order that you can have a focussed approach to ensuring you are addressing the right part of you that needs to change, that is, your Character and its battle with Sin.

If you are a Christian, then abide in Him. As you abide in Him consider thoughts that arise and ask yourself if they are legitimate needs of your body or Personality? Do they match the Character of Christ? Or is this sin at work in you? This is a very helpful discipline on your walk with Jesus as you look to be transformed into His image. 2 Corinthians 3, v18.

God bless you on your journey.

Focus on letting Christ be Himself in you: -

Red corner: -	Be grafted into Christ, abide in Him, put on the armour of Christ and check which bit of you is motivating your behaviour.
Green corner: -	Talk with Christ in you by His Holy Spirit and listen and do what he says.
Blue corner: -	God will create a unique journey for you as you play your part in His Church.
Yellow corner: -	Follow the process of discipleship well and you will be able to look back and see He has made a path for you.
Central: -	Jesus is both passionate and balanced in all He does and He expects you to produce spiritual fruit, even if it is just a grape sized fruit.

15

Applications

From the examples in the book, you can see many ways that this approach can be helpful. The following examples are there to reinforce the opportunities that exist by thinking in this way.

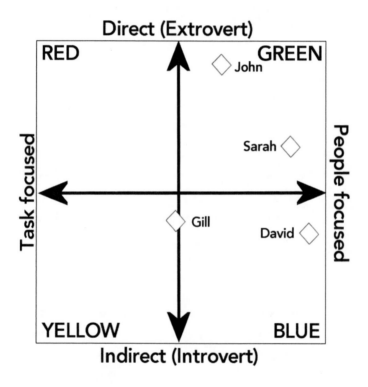

The Birkman Map®

The Coffee Team

In the map above, you can see that there are four members of the church coffee team who serve after the church meeting.

- Can you guess the sorts of Strengths this team might have?

- Can you guess the sort of problems the church might have with them?

- Who would be the best person to ensure the ordering of supplies?

- Generally speaking, this coffee team are likely to be good at dealing with people, especially Sarah and David. John is not shy, so he is likely to do well at engaging visitors and ensuring the team is energised.

- None of the team are especially task focused, so actually getting people to stop talking and take their coffee might be an issue. Long queue-lines are likely.

- Gill is not especially task focused or good at process, however, she is probably more likely than her three team-mates to ensure the supplies are ordered and ready each week.

Of course, having the right Personality mix is helpful, but that will not help if they are a miserable or uncaring bunch of people. The right mix of Personality with Christ's Character shining through will serve people very well.

The Worship Team

The next map is of Worship Team B who serves the church alternate Sundays.

- Which members of the team are likely to present an energetic face when the team is leading?
- Which members of the team are likely to engage best with reflective songs?
- What sort of problems is this team likely to struggle with?

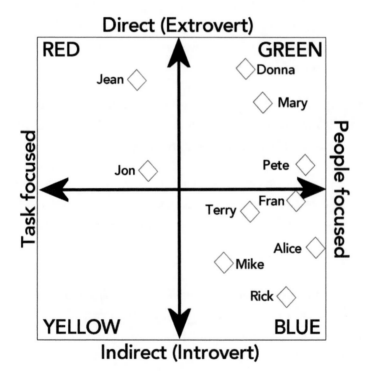

The Birkman Map®

- Jean, Donna and Mary are likely to present an energetic face when they are serving along with perhaps Jon and Pete.

- Rick and perhaps Mike and Alice are likely to engage best with reflective songs along with perhaps Terry and Fran.

- This team has a bias towards people rather than tasks, therefore they may struggle getting things done practically. The team has no structured or administration type of people, so it might not be well organised. There might not be anyone standing up for tradition, which can leave a gap in the way the team functions.

Having a team that is balanced is likely to be more effective in leading the Church worship. But without Christ's Character and gifting, without listening to the prompting of the Holy Spirit, then the team are just a music group.

The Church Leadership Team

This medium sized church has two full time leaders, John and Phillip, their map is over the page: -

- What Strengths is John likely to add to this team?
- What Strengths is Phillip likely to bring to the team?
- In what way is this team likely to be biased?
- What problems might this church have, because of this team?
- What can be done, to Strengthen this team?

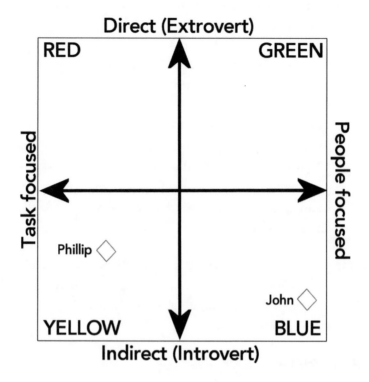

The Birkman Map®

- John is likely to be thoughtful, creative and focused on the future. He will probably enjoy the word and perhaps the music and aesthetics of things in the church.

- Phillip is likely to be much more structured and organised than John, have a good historical perspective and like John, be quite reflective and thoughtful.

- This team of two is likely to be seen as quiet and reflective, perhaps a little reserved and may be focused on the word, prayer and contemplation.

- This church might struggle with outreach and the more active expressions of worship. The church may find it hard to pro-actively engage with the community.

- Adding leaders to the team that are much more direct and love to engage people will help give a stronger emphasis on outreach work, as well as improve communication generally. Adding a very practical person may help to get things done more quickly and effectively and avoid procrastinating, which the team might be prone too.

Digging in the damp patch

You cannot of course, make definite decisions about a team based on the evidence from such a map as we have just looked at. You have to talk with people, but it is a good place to start.

If you're looking for water in the desert, then you just don't dig everywhere, you look for a 'damp patch', a place where something may already be growing, or there has been evidence of water in the past. Once you find such a place, then you dig and dig and then dig some more, to see if your reasonable suspicions are true. If you are right, then you will find water.

When you look at John in the above map, it is reasonable to assume he is thoughtful and reserved, so I would ask questions that dig into this area and explore this. It may be that John is very self-aware and works really hard to be more active and directive than his Blue Personality suggests. By digging into this damp patch, you can quickly find out how self-aware someone is; are they comfortable with their Personality, striving to be like someone else, or consciously adapting their behaviour to make up for gaps in the team? Every case is different. Many teams I have worked with have not admitted to each other the areas where they are not strong and therefore these areas are not explored at all. I usually find people know there is an issue, but cannot find a way of safely talking about it.

My interventions aim to safely bring to the surface such issues. The fact that it is OK to be the person God made you to be is part of this. If God has planted you into the place of leadership, He has also probably given you people to balance out your Strengths, but unless you talk about these things, they can remain quite hidden.

Making it safe

No matter whether you are meeting as friends, leaders or the Board, there is one key issue that applies to all. People generally only say what they think when they feel safe.

Feeling safe is the biggest obstacle to people working well together. As soon as you feel unsafe then your brain releases chemicals, which leads to the production of adrenalin. This floods your body in order to get it ready to run away or stand and fight. One consequence is that your brain is starved of blood as more blood is sent to your heart, liver and muscles and so it becomes much harder to think and much easier to run or fight.

Now as we have become much more civilised, we also have generally learnt to be more sophisticated. Therefore, our response is better described as moving into silence or verbal violence. This is explored really well in the book 'Crucial Conversations', (Patterson et al, McGraw-Hill Contemporary, 2002) which I highly recommend.

Silence is being absent from a conversation and not saying what you really think, which leads to de-motivation and disengagement. Violence, on the other hand, can be dismissive, destructive, sarcastic, or plain aggressive. The aim of course, is to talk safely about your Strengths and differences, but there is a way of bringing safety in order to facilitate such conversations. This includes focusing on the common goal or purpose that the team is working on, this leads to developing mutual respect and eventually mutual trust for one another by valuing and honouring each other. Finding a common goal is easy as we have a clear mutual purpose in glorifying God through all we do, and working to be in obedience to what God wants for us.

I was very privileged to have lunch with Dr Birkman a few years ago. I asked him what he thought was the biggest obstacle to engaging with people, in order to help them to understand themselves and others. His reply was as I suspected. He said, "Fear - fear of embarrassment, fear of being vulnerable - fear is what most people struggle with."

Making it safe by the removal of fear is the key to releasing genuine honest relationships. The antidote to fear is love as John wrote in his first letter,

> *So we have known and believe the love that God has for us. God is love, and those who abide in love abide in God, and God abides in them. Love has been perfected among us in this: that we may have boldness on the day of judgement, because as he is, so are we in this world. There is no*

fear in love, but perfect love casts out fear; for fear has to do with punishment, and whoever fears has not reached perfection in love. We love because he first loved us. Those who say, "I love God," and hate their brothers or sisters, are liars; for those who do not love a brother or sister whom they have seen, cannot love God whom they have not seen. The commandment we have from him is this: those who love God must love their brothers and sisters also.

1 John. 4 v16-21

One-man ministry

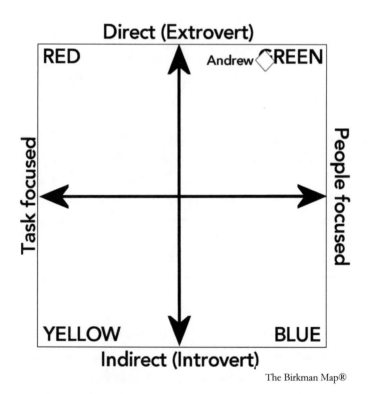

The Birkman Map®

What then do you do, if you find you are alone in leadership? Let's take the example of Andrew in the map above. We can assume that Andrew is likely to be loud, energetic, a good communicator, people focused and persuasive, and likes to win.

In leading his church, we can expect to find energetic outreach, good community engagement and people who know what is going on, because Andrew will tell them. Andrew is very Green. If he tries to lead on his own, it would not be long until he wears everyone else out. The worship might be a bit of a loud affair. In truth he is probably not very musical or very practical, being some way from both the Blue and the Red corners of the map. When it comes to being well organised and carefully planned, he probably has next to no understanding of what that means. It is simply not him.

Andrew can either lead a very lopsided, energetic and exciting church until it burns up with exhaustion or he can work at building a team around him. He has to find the people that God has given him that can fill the Red, Blue and Yellow gaps that he does not have. The hardest task for him will be finding a Yellow person, because he hardly understands what it is to be Yellow. However, if he starts by finding a Red and Blue person to build with, then they can help him find a Yellow person, because they will at least understand something of what it is to be Yellow.

One Green leader I know has, on two occasions, appointed a church administrator that he believed was strongly Yellow, an organised and process driven person. But in truth, both times, they were barely in the Yellow part of the map. He just can't see that far across the map himself, so what he sees as Yellow is barely Yellow. Maybe next time he will get the rest of the team to be more vocal in the interview process.

No matter what your colour is, it is hard to serve a church with all types of people and keep them all engaged. The people next to you, horizontally and vertically on the map, are easier for you to understand and engage with them. However, generally speaking people who are diagonal opposite from your colour, are the hardest for you to understand and successfully engage with.

What about people who are close to the centre? To a degree, such people are in a good place to engage others from each colour of the map. In fact in business, central people can make good general managers or CEOs and you can expect them to make effective church leaders. However, they cannot see right into the corners of each area. So if you are very Red, very Green, very Yellow or very Blue, then a central person may well struggle to understand and engage with you. This can damp-down extreme extroverts and ignore extreme introverts completely. However, God calls people from every part of the map and He therefore expects leadership to engage with all types of people. The only man who is both central and yet big enough to fully understand all the extremes of the map is Jesus Himself.

Jesus is the only one-man ministry that ever worked perfectly as God intended. If you find you are the only person leading a church, then build a team round you. There is an old saying, *"A single stick is easily broken, but a bundle of sticks is remarkably strong". (Aesop)*

Worship trap

A typical worship group can also fall in to a 'bias trap'. For example, people with Blue Needs and Strengths, (who are insightful, reflective and tend to have a small select group of friends) tend to like to spend time with other Blue people.

This can lead to a Blue worship leader unconsciously forming a band of other Blue people around them. I believe this is a key part of the reason that cliques are formed - people of the same Personality colour tend to like each other's company.

Musical Interest is a Blue trait and therefore many worship leaders are typically Blue. Because they are naturally comfortable with people from the same colour group, they can subconsciously form a Blue worship group.

However, a Blue group is likely to select contemplative songs that are not high-energy, directive or declarative. They may really enjoy endless cycles of chord progressions, which allows lots of time for reflection and soaking in the music.

I have observed one very Blue worship leader who was asked not to play his guitar endlessly between songs in order to allow silence for God to speak and others to contribute. Even though he was asked by the church leader several times, he just couldn't stop himself from endless cycles of chords because it felt right to him. He was stuck in a 'Blue bubble' that assumes that if it was good for him, it must be good for everyone.

I have also met very Yellow worship leaders, who if they do not have the music in front of them, they cannot play the song. Improvisation is not how music is written so they tend not to improvise. Because they are attracted to people like themselves they can gather other Yellow musicians and create a rather rigid worship team, without any space for creativity at all - it is even a stretch to get a chorus repeated as it is not written that way.

Imagine a worship group made of only Red people, or only Green people. You can imagine how unbalanced they would be. I worked with one Green worship leader who led through his forcefulness; he often didn't learn the words to songs and would make up the words as he went. It was like being at a football match, lots of energy but very hard to follow.

God made each of us unique and when we understand these differences we can ensure that all the Strengths are included. This avoids us creating teams that are distorted or lopsided. It does of course require some effort in learning and applying the lessons of the map, in order to avoid falling in to the single colour trap.

Building the Church together

One way that you can use Personality information is with mutual discipleship, be that with two or three friends or as part of a small group. We provide a course called 'Authentic Community', which enables small groups of people to discover together, some insights about each of their personalities (you can find details in appendix 4).

This gives a focus for genuine conversation about how God made each of you unique and how we can adapt to support one another.

One example is a quiet person named Catherine whose workbook said 'while she appears quiet, she will have an opinion if you ask her'. The rest of the group asked if this was true. "I am happy to listen and take in all your different opinions," Catherine affirmed, "but if you don't ask, I will probably stay silent. I don't want to be rude and push in with my thoughts". From that point onwards one of the group always made sure she asked what Catherine was thinking, which meant they had much more dynamic group conversations.

Personality is not enough

Understanding your Personality, celebrating how God made you, and recognising how He made others different from you, is helpful, but it is not enough on its own.

Take the example of Sarah, who is in her mid-twenties and is usually a Green extrovert with lots of Blue Interests and Needs. If we look at just her Personality, then we can see this bright and bubbly person, who is a good singer, with a warm smile, good bible knowledge and excellent communication skills and organised just enough and therefore appears to makes an excellent worship leader. She leads exciting worship, with which the church engages well. She is popular with the church and with the leadership team.

Yet her relationship with a young man who she was convinced was 'the one for her' has just ended. The reason is a mystery to her, but obvious to the young man. Sarah has a great Personality and good knowledge of the Bible; she is clearly a Christian and is sensitive to the Holy Spirit. However, her knowledge of God and the Bible has not grown into belief, or grown further into a value, or formed a central attitude of who she is. She has not yet developed a Character like Christ's.

- Knowledge alone does not change anything

- Knowledge that is believed starts to make a difference to our Character

- Belief is a choice

- A belief that we associate with important values shapes our Character and therefore our behaviour

- Knowledge that we believe and has become part of our value system becomes ingrained overtime into an attitude; it becomes part of our Character, part of who we are.

Sarah remains self-centred and insecure. She constantly seeks reassurance from those close to her and all of her relationships are about her need to be loved and accepted. This reveals original sin at work in her, it is self-centred not God centred. It shows that she is not trusting God or finding rest in the assurance that she is loved by God. In the end, her self-centredness drove the young man away. Her great Personality is not enough; she needs a great Character as well.

If Sarah had pastoral teaching and support that helped her understand and believe the truth of the gospel (Romans. 5); the assurance that comes with faith (Hebrews. 11), the promise of the Holy Spirit (John. 14), the freedom that Christ has set her free (Galatians .5), the truth that she is an heir in Christ (Galatians. 3), that she is credited with His righteousness (Romans. 4) and this list is just a short extract of the truth, then her insecurity and needy behaviour can be addressed.

What Sarah needs is pastoral help to both celebrate the Personality God has given her and at the same time help her to have Christ living in her. Sarah needs Jesus in her, to help her make choices about her own Character so that it will be like Christ's Character. Her self-centredness is something she has learnt, amplified by sin and now she needs to unlearn, but it is hard to do this alone, which is why we have the Church and the Holy Spirit.

Imagine Sarah's great Personality with a Character that was confident, secure and at peace with God in the same way that Christ is. This is what Sarah needs and what her Pastoral oversight needs to be helping her with.

Sarah's Personality with Christ's Character.

Sarah needs to be herself in Jesus and have Jesus being Himself in her.

16

Final thoughts

Understanding yourself

I hope that through this book you have gained some insight into the individual Personality Needs and Interests that God gave you and how this makes you different from everyone around you. Working through this book means that you will have been able to guess much about your God-given Personality. While this is helpful, it is not a substitute for being accurately measured with an assessment.

Understanding yourself is important, but equally important is the understanding of how people are different from you. The map is a good shorthand way of using this information every day. That way you can adapt how you behave, to get the best from others as well as explaining your Needs, which will help others get the best from you.

Knowing yourself however, is not an excuse for poor behaviour. It is not acceptable to say "I have a low literary score so I can't be asked to write this report". Instead, say "I have a low literary score so I struggle with writing which I find tiring, therefore I am going to break it into more manageable chunks and then ensure I get re-energised in between".

Brothers united?

In Luke. 15 v11-32, Jesus told a story of a father and his two sons. We do not know much about the Personality of the two brothers, as the story is focussed on their Character and that of their father. We see that it is their Character that is flawed.

The younger son may have been a Green Personality. We know he liked being sociable, he seems to have persuaded his father to give him his inheritance before the father's death and he may have seen the inheritance as a win. He certainly did not use it to plan for the future; rather he immediately went out and enjoyed life. Before long, the inheritance was spent.

The older son was dutiful and focused on the hard work of the field; in fact, he worked so hard that he felt like he was his father's slave. His clear task focus and his sense of authority, suggests he may have been rather Red and his stubbornness might imply he may have been Yellow. What we do know is that his Personality was somewhat different from his brother's. When he learned that his lost brother had returned, he could hear music and dancing from the house and found out his father had killed the fattened calf, was in his Character that he was angry and stubborn.

We can see sin was at work amplifying the younger son's Personality into a selfish, inconsiderate Character that had no understanding, respect, honour or love for his family, leading to him wasting his inheritance.

The older brother is no better, with sin amplifying his task nature into a sense of slavery and his authority into anger and stubbornness.

His reaction to his lost brother's return showed no love for his brother or father.

It is only when we look at the father, who thought his younger son was dead and then finds he is alive, that we start to understand the story. He is a man who values love of people above things. He is neither selfish nor angry or stubborn. He had his priorities right. He saw relationship as more important than punishing his children.

This story helps us to focus on what God, our Father, is about. Love. It shows that while Personality may be influenced by sin and a Character can form that is selfish or angry, love can overcome all and forgive all. Our Father loves in such a way that love, through forgiveness and grace, opens the way to restoring our relationship with Him through Christ.

We can all learn that when brothers and sisters take the lead from their heavenly Father's vision of love and grace, then relationships can be restored and people can be together, in love, honouring the Father and His vision of love for all peoples.

Be the person God wants you to be, a fixed, God-given Personality with a malleable Character that is being changed to be like Christ.

Appendices

Appendix 1

'Being myself in Jesus'

Being myself is not half so bad as I thought that it might be.
Living in the love of Jesus, who loves the likes of me.
And isn't it good to know, I don't even have to try,
To fight for a place in this old human race, since I'm already home and dry.
Phewwww!

Seems to me that the things I like are the things I can do without,
Seems to me that the things I hate are the things in which I fail.
'N isn't it good to know, there's someone who understands,
When I give up He still loves me as much as when I'm doing the best I can.

> So I'm being myself in Jesus and He's being Himself in me.
> I'm being myself in Jesus and that's the way to be.
> I'm being myself in Jesus and He's being Himself in me.
> And the life that He gives is the life that I live and I'm living it naturally.

So many times I have tried to be something that I'm really not.
Thinking so much of the things I lack, I forget the things I've got,
Yet it's so hard to take, when the image comes tumbling down,
God gives you grace when you're put in your place, down on your face on the ground.

So I'm being myself in Jesus and He's being Himself in me.
I'm being myself in Jesus and that's the way to be.
I'm being myself in Jesus and He's being Himself in me
And the life that He gives is the life that I live and I'm living it naturally.

If I should say what I really feel, O would you laugh at me?
If I should show my weaknesses, would you walk all over me?
If you should find the real me, tell me would you turn me down?
Please tell me No, Keep my confidence growing, in this family love I found.

'Cos I'm being myself in Jesus and He's being Himself in me.
I'm being myself in Jesus and that's the way to be.
I'm being myself in Jesus and He's being Himself in me.
And the life that He gives is the life that I live and I'm living it naturally.

Appendix 2

How to engage with, accept and love your God-given Personality.

1. Thank God for the Personality He has given you.

2. Give thanks for your Interests and consider how they are, or could be, working in your life.

3. Give thanks for your God-given Needs and your Strengths especially where your Strengths match your Needs.

4. Ask God to speak with you about your learnt Strengths. Recognise that while they may be successful, they will not meet your Needs. Seek God's help in allowing you, where you can, to relax back towards your more natural Strengths that will meet your God-given Needs.

5. Ask God to show you opportunities to put your energy into the Interests and natural Strengths God has given you.

6. Ask God to show you how to let go of roles that will drain you dry, if you have no choice but to undertake that role, complement it with an Interest that energises you.

7. If God presents you with a person in need, in the way He did with the Good Samaritan, then do your best in that moment. Know when you have done enough and pass the matter on to someone else who is better designed to deal with the issue.

8. Be honest about your Needs. Let people know what you Need, so that they have the opportunity to adapt their behaviour to better meet your Needs. They may want you to shine, but are blinded by their own perceptual filters. So tell them lovingly and gently, how God made you to Need certain things, that are different from them.

9. Being forgetful is part of life, so if other people forget your Needs then tell them again, because other people will default to their own Strengths and forget what you Need. Being forgetful is not a sin, it is a reality of life that grows with age.

10. Don't be hard on yourself, if past decisions turn out to be a bad match for your Personality. Parents, teachers, advisors and society, generally do not know what is best for you, but they usually do try the as hard as they can. Whether your Strengths are natural or developed through what you have learnt, then delight in them.

Appendix 3

How to invite Christ to be Himself in you

In order to ensure Christ is living in you, there are some key areas to keep in mind: -

- Be grafted in to Christ through accepting salvation.

- Abide in Christ by drinking the spiritual food and drink that rises through the 'sap' of being grafted into Him.

- Ask the Holy Spirit to live in you and be eager to receive the Spirit's prompting throughout every day.

- Put on the full armour of God: - the belt of truth, the breastplate of His righteousness, the gospel of peace, the shield of faith, the helmet of Salvation and the sword of the Spirit the word of God.

Abiding in Christ: -

1. At all times ask The Holy Spirit to speak to you. Listen and respond.

2. Pray.

3. Praise, thank and worship Him.

4. Read His word and ask The Holy Spirit to speak through the word.

5. Bring His words to the front of your mind daily.

6. Talk with other Christians to learn more about Christ.

7. Read good authors who expand the word of God, but always test it back to the Bible itself.

8. Remove distractions by asking God to show you where you are investing time and energy into something that is a waste.

9. Turn your focus to listen to God, through The Spirit and through His word.

10. God is your Father, Jesus is your brother and the Spirit is your strength, power, comforter and guide. Each aspect of God wants to speak into your life and to shape your Character.

Abide in Christ and be conscious of your Personality and Character

The above are clear steps that we can each take daily because of His love. However, I would propose the following steps, based on our understanding that we have a body, a God-given Personality, a Character we want to change to be like Christ and an ongoing battle with sin.

In life, at every choice you have to make, at every decision, whenever you take an action you can follow these steps: -

1. Ask yourself the question. Is the issue before you, simply your physical body presenting a desire? If yes, what is the appropriate response?

    Or is the issue more than your body speaking?

2. Ask yourself the question. Is the issue, being driven by your God-given Personality's Interests or Needs? If yes, what is the appropriate response?

    Or is the issue more than your body and your Personality speaking?

3. Ask yourself the question. Does your planned behaviour agree with and conform to, the expectations and truths about Jesus' Character? If not, then your belief, value or attitude is flawed. Ask

The Holy Spirit to renew your mind so that your Character will reflect Christ's Character. This is when you need Christ's Character in you, you need Jesus to be Himself in you. Ask Him to be Lord of the moment, Lord of your choice, Lord of your behaviour. It will require strength in order to do the right thing, so ask the Holy Spirit for strength and He will give it.

Or is the issue more than your body and your Personality speaking and an incorrect Character at work?

4. Then ask yourself the question. Are you being tempted to act in a way that is rooted in the selfishness of sin in you? If yes, then you know that you need God's help in order to choose the right behaviour. "This is the battle with sin, it is not like a battle, it **is** a battle".

Appendix 4

- An 8-week course for groups of three or four people to discover more about themselves and each other.

- Designed to enable people to share safely together.

- Each individual person gets their own unique workbook containing statements about themselves.

- Discover how to build stronger friendships in your church through sharing the tailor made statements about you.

- Get more reality and depth into your relationships.

- Cultivate meaningful friendships through this aid to authenticity.

Visit   www.insightsfor.org   for more information.

About the Author

Colin became a Christian in his late teens and over the last 40 years has served the Church in many roles, including Worship Leader, Treasurer and Trustee, as well as a Church and Pastoral Team Leader as part of the eldership team in his local Church.

He is a director of "insightsfor.org", which provides high quality leadership and personal development resources to churches, Christian organisations, charities and individuals.

His first career was for 25 years, initially in Nursing, then in general management. He then became a freelance Management Consultant, mentor and personal coach. He has worked with individuals and teams in a variety of settings, in I.T. Sales, Charities and Churches, assisting with conflict resolution, personal coaching and personal and team development.

He is a Birkman Master Certified Professional and has worked with Birkman International Inc. since 2004. He has a pastor's heart that longs to encourage and nurture, and he delights in the growth of others.

As Colin himself says, "the most significant learning for me has been the understanding that God made each of us unique and different. These differences, that often drive us apart, are the same differences that complement us, if we only knew it." He is the author of the unique 8-week "Authentic Community" workbooks, which gives insight into the uniqueness of each individual's Personality and enables the development of real, transparent and open relationships within church small groups.

Colin and his wife Mandie live in Devon, UK, from where they keep in close touch with their 4 children and 2 grandchildren.

Addendum

Key message, a plea to church leaders

During the editing and review process of this book, it has become increasingly clear to readers that it contains a message that addresses a very real need in our churches. With this in mind I have been encouraged to write this specific message to church leaders. It's a message about how we can better honour and value each other and the differences we find in all our people. This book speaks to how we can better use these differences to further the Kingdom, and build a better expression here on earth of who God really is. This will in turn help us to guard against unnecessary division and hurt.

As a church leader, you already know how to handle the Bible. You would not rely on a single source when considering the Bible, or just use one commentary. Reading one author is helpful; getting the different points of view from several authors helps us get a greater perspective and a much deeper understanding. We each want to ensure that we stay sharp with a clear focus, by sharpening iron with iron (Proverbs. 27 v17).

In this book, I argue that relating to different people is remarkably similar. We naturally think our way of dealing with people is the best way.

We need to understand how each individual perspective is different from the next and sometimes very different. More importantly, our view might not be the best or most effective view.

Understanding these differences is not enough, because we are called to understand, accept, engage with, honour and love, all the different personalities in those people God puts with us.

I have heard Church Leaders make statements that, when considered, are very damaging to people: -

"God has just not given me the right people".

Sub-text:- You are the wrong people.

"We need to focus on the next generation"

Sub-text:- I will only use people aged under 30.

"We need people of Character, so we are bringing in a leader from elsewhere".

Sub-text:- I can't find people of Character amongst you.

Such statements (and there are plenty more), damage the people in our churches, sometimes permanently, and this often means we exclude or dismiss people for the wrong reasons.

When Nehemiah rebuilt the walls, he used the material that God had given him, burnt wood and stones and **all** the people, sword in one hand trowel in the other.

A key message in this book is that every person God gives us in our churches has got something positive to bring. It is up to us as leaders to discover why God has given us each person and how they can contribute.

There are a number of ways we can do this: -

1. Give thanks to God for each and every one.

2. Consider how you can value, honour, and to some degree understand each one.

3. Remember, Christ paid the same price for each person that He paid for you. We are all equally valuable.

4. Do not assume that their Personality is like yours. It is not, each one is uniquely different.

5. If they are saved, assume that their Character does reflect something of Christ.

6. If they make a mistake, don't punish them, but bring them correction with the forgiveness and restoration that is the heart of the Gospel and help them to change by His Spirit to be more like Christ.

7. Be like the father of the prodigal son and when someone returns to their spiritual life, welcome them, have a party, and show them the Fathers' love.

8. If someone is a wolf of course you must protect the flock, but there are not many wolves (Matthew. 7 v15)!

9. Accept, value, honour and love all of the people God has given you. Then you will start to see the multifaceted Glory of Jesus reflected a little more in each one and you will see the church better reflect God in all His fullness.

His intent was that now, through the church, the manifold wisdom of God should be made known to the rulers and authorities in the heavenly realms, according to his eternal purpose that he accomplished in Christ Jesus our Lord.

Ephesians. 3 v10.

10. Learn the lessons in this book, so that you can understand how you can speak effectively to the full range of personalities in your church. Learn to delight in the diversity God has given you and how you can work together as the teams God has intended for you, so that you can better display the fullness of His Glory here on earth.

I pray that the truth in this book will expand your understanding of God's people and you will build the church to His Glory.

Yours in Christ,

Colin.

Blank pages for your notes.

Blank pages for your notes.

|

Blank pages for your notes.

Blank pages for your notes.

Blank pages for your notes.

Blank pages for your notes.

Blank pages for your notes.

Blank pages for your notes.

Blank pages for your notes.